Art
Is All Around Us

Art
Is All Around Us

Rubye Mae Griffith

Photographs by Arnold Wall

South Brunswick and New York: A. S. Barnes and Company
London: Thomas Yoseloff Ltd

A.S. Barnes and Co., Inc.
Cranbury, New Jersey 08512

Thomas Yoseloff Ltd
108 New Bond Street
London W1Y OQX, England

SBN 498 06960 5
Printed in the United States of America

TO THE YOUNG IN ART—
WHATEVER THEIR AGE

Contents

Introduction: Art versus Non-Art

The purpose of this book is to encourage non-artists to become artists.

The book sets out to prove that art is everywhere and that everyone may enjoy art, learn to appreciate art, and thus become more sensitive to the beauty of the world in which we live.

Adults as well as young people will derive equal benefit from the book—provided they approach its pages WITHOUT BIAS.

We believe that one way of helping the reader to do this is to erase the semantic distinction that has so long been drawn between the "artist" and the "artisan."

The artisan has been defined as one possessing manual or mechanical dexterity; the artist as one who displays ability in the "fine arts"—so called because they require "tastefulness" and "scientific knowledge."

To this we say: "RUBBISH!"

It doesn't matter in the least whether you possess manual or mechanical dexterity, tastefulness or scientific knowledge. If you have feelings, and we assume that you do, you are potentially artistic.

If you write a poem, compose a melody, invent a new dance, or paint a picture, you are saying how you feel about life and this expression of feeling makes you an artist.

Many people will deny this. In fact, most people will.

These are the people who insist that in order to become an artist you must submit to training and discipline; you must abide by definite rules and you must follow established principles.

To this we say: "Agreed!"—if you wish to become a professional or a commercial artist. If you want to write or paint or dance or sing IN ORDER TO MAKE MONEY OR TO BECOME FAMOUS, then you must conform to the standards set by others and you must express yourself IN A WAY THAT

WILL PLEASE OTHERS.

To do this you will have to study and strive to "perfect" your art.

But the sad fact is, you will never perfect it.

You may distort it, inhibit it, commercialize it, give it slickness, sophistication, and popular appeal; but then it will no longer be YOUR art for it will not express YOUR feelings.

However, in supressing your feelings and adapting your artistic expression to the approval of others you may wind up rich. And you may wind up famous.

If this is the reward you seek, go after it. With persistence and perseverence you should attain it. But in doing so you will lose something very precious. You will lose the pure, unadulterated, heart-singing, head-spinning JOY OF SELF-EXPRESSION!

If this doesn't matter to you; if you want to become a rich, famous, FRUSTRATED ARTIST, set this book aside. It is very definitely not your dish of tea.

Instead of inspiring you it will simply annoy you.

But, if you earnestly long to appreciate the beauty and wonder and order of life; if you want to train your eye and your mind to find design everywhere—in the humblest and lowliest objects as well as in the most awesome—if you want to express your feelings about life through your hands or your paintbrush; if you want to release your tensions, sublimate your hostilities, exorcise your fears and, at the same time, gain a glorious sense of accomplishment, then by all means read on, because this book is for you.

Whether you are a teenager, a toddler, a teacher, a therapist, a housewife, a mature citizen or just a dabbler, you will find, in this book, ways to make your life richer, your heart lighter, your outlook brighter.

Within the pages of this book you will learn how, with the barest possible expenditure and the scantiest right-at-hand materials, you can bring fresh purpose and meaning into your life.

For the exhilarating, soul-lifting fact is that the ART *IS* ALL AROUND US.

There is beauty in paper clips, milk cartons, distributor caps, and cotton swabs; in toothpicks, toilet floats, and tin cans; in bits of string, broken glass, and bent nails!

In fact, the stimulus for artistic expression may be found at the supermarket, the hardware store, in the medicine chest, or at the rummage sale.

The important thing is to begin the lifelong search for beauty; for wherever we seek it, we find it.

And once we learn to find design, order, and beauty in the trivia of life, we move up the ladder of art appreciation to discover beauty in the world's great paintings, books, plays, and operas.

The writer of this book has demonstrated, in her own experience, that it is possible to enjoy the thrill of artistic expression and to convey that thrill to others without benefit of formal instruction.

She taught herself to paint in oil, tempera, and casein. She learned, unassisted, to work in clay and opened her own successful ceramic studio. She has worked in leather, metal, wood, and plastics and she has composed songs that were published, though she cannot read a note of music.

Therefore she believes she has earned the right to call herself an artistic non-artist.

She must, however, make two points very clear.

The first is that self-instruction can never take the place of formal instruction FOR THOSE WHO WISH TO BECOME PROFESSIONALS IN THEIR FIELD.

The second point is that many of the world's highly revered artists became fine artists in spite of formal instruction—this because they refused to allow the methods or the opinions of others to inhibit their feelings or their own mode of artistic expression.

And that is actually the whole premise of this little "Primer For Primitives." It is meant to be a help and a guide to those non-artists who may never win the world's approval or the title of "artist," but who nevertheless will have more fun than anyone with their "Non-Art."

Art
Is All Around Us

1

Where Do You Start?

Where do you start in your search for art? You start where you are with what you have. You look within and you listen. Then you follow the promptings you hear. But you steel yourself to disregard the advice, the criticism, and the suggestions of well-intentioned, well-meaning friends.

How do I know this is true? Because this is what I did. And, in doing so, I became an artist. Now, mind you, not a rich artist and not a famous artist. But a happy, fulfilled and appreciated artist. And I'm hoping that you will do likewise.

I don't wish to bore you with details from my private life. But there are some experiences I must share with you simply because I believe that in doing so I may be able to lead you down the path of self discovery as an artist. So please bear with me if I describe that path as I followed it.

For more than twenty years I secretly longed to express myself through some medium of art. I never openly expressed this longing because I feared others would laugh at it. Still the desire persisted. And eventually I decided I must do something about it.

Throughout this time I earned my living in advertising and had no time for the study or pursuit of art. Now I'm glad that things happened this way. For if my artistic longing had been satisfied, if I had received formal instruction in art and mastered formal techniques, I not only would never have experienced the truly remarkable thrill of becoming an artist, unaided, but I would not have been able to help you to experience the same wonderful thrill of accomplishment.

How Do You Begin?

Now you know where you start. You start with you. With the trembling and tenuous feeling that tells you you have something to say about life. Deep within you there is tension and turmoil and tenderness, so carefully concealed beneath matter-of-factness and busyness that even your closest associates fail to suspect their existence. But you know that they must have out.

The important thing is not to discuss these feelings with anyone. If you do you will be counseled, directed, perhaps even silenced. And how pitiable this would be. For then all these stifled urgings would remain stifled. And if any were given air or space to grow in they might be controlled or distorted by others and then they would not become expressions of the real you at all.

So what you must do, the way you must begin, is to set aside a few precious private moments every day for self-discovery.

Can you do this once a week? Or oftener? You alone can decide. Maybe you'll wind up with an hour. A half hour. Fifteen minutes. No matter!

Start with five minutes if you must. Only start!

You'll soon find that more time will become available. Why? Because, however trite the statement may sound, we find time to do the things that we want to do. And so you will find time for creative self-expression IF YOU REALLY WANT TO EXPRESS YOURSELF.

What About Materials, Etc.?

And now we will assume that you have pushed aside family or friends or general busyness long enough to have won for yourself this luxurious "you" time.

This is the time you will use to find yourself as an artist and as a person. Now what materials or supplies will you need to acquire in order to use your time profitably?

Actually all you need, at first is some place to sit quietly and think. It can be indoors or outdoors; a quiet place or even a noisy one, if there is no other; for we can always establish quiet within ourselves, even in the midst of noise, if we have to.

Of course the pleasanter our surroundings and the more room we have to spread out in and leave our "makings" undisturbed between creative sessions, the better. But we aren't going to wait for perfect circumstances or surroundings.

I waited for over twenty years and accomplished nothing.

Oh, I know some of us have to wait for careers to terminate or families to grow up or finances to improve or for all sorts of problems to be solved. But there will always come a time, that now-is-the-moment time, when you know if you don't do it now you never will and that's the moment when you sit down quietly and think.

You think what do I really want to do, in an artistic sense, that I've never done before because I thought I couldn't, or shouldn't, or wouldn't be able to?

Have you longed to paint with tempera or water color or oils?

Have you wished you could let yourself go with color, dynamic, outspoken, soul-surging color?

Have you wondered what you could make with your hands?

And are you suddenly stopped in your wondering by the thought that you may have to buy costly materials, assemble an awesome array of jars, brushes, easels, canvases, instruction books, and so on?

Well, we can quiet that fear. Because you don't have to buy anything. Not at first. Later you may want to buy art supplies or craft materials. But that's later. Such things aren't really expensive. And you won't mind going without something you once considered important in order to buy them. Because nothing will seem more important to you than your new-found freedom and your thrilling creative experiments.

But in the beginning, when you are just starting out, when you are trying to find yourself as a person and discover what sort of artistic expression gives you the most personal satisfaction, JUST REACH OUT FOR WHATEVER COMES TO HAND.

That's what I do.

It may be paper clips or paper fasteners; yarn scraps or fabric remnants; dried coffee grounds or colored eggshells; flour and water and food coloring; bent nails or discarded hardware. It may, in fact, be anything in this wild, wide, wonderful world—animal, vegetable or mineral!

You see, it isn't what it is but what you do with it and what it does for you that counts.

You take these fabric scraps or navy beans or paper doilies or bobby pins or old cans of house paint and you sit down with them and you relax and you let the materials lead you on a voyage of self-discovery.

You don't say I will make this or that or do thus and such.

You spread your materials out on a contrasting surface—put light materials on a dark surface or dark materials on a light surface—and you let them tell you what they want to become.

It will seem, as you do this, that the materials acquire a life of their own and, through a process of self-determination, turn into all sorts of amazing, pleasing designs, independently of your volition.

But quite the reverse is true.

The Artist In You

There is a creative power within you that creates artistically when you allow it to do so. This power works best, as you do yourself, when you are permissive toward it, when you encourage it and give it free rein.

As soon as you interpose your inhibitions, restraints, and uncertainties in any creative situation you get in the way of this power. This is also true when you attempt to copy someone else's work instead of creating your own. And it is true when you try to please someone else other than yourself or attempt to win his approval of your work.

I can't explain why this is so and I doubt whether anyone else can. It just happens that way, as any truly creative teacher or psychologist will tell you.

The amazing thing to me is that I knew this to be true in the field of writing, for I had experienced the results of this truth in my work as an advertising writer, where I not only created many successful advertising campaigns but also originated many popular and effective musical commercials.

Whenever I tried to write to please someone else or to win approval, whenever I attempted to force my writing or to direct it, ideas came haltingly and were seldom acceptable.

But if I wrote freely, seeking only to please myself; if I simply put a piece of paper in the typewriter, convinced that something would appear on it, and put down whatever ideas happened to come to me, I found the ideas arrived in ever-increasing quantity and their quality was always exceptional.

I followed this principle of free-flowing creativity in my writing for more than twenty years, and never, in all that time, was there ever a lack of ideas. Many ideas had to be cast aside as impractical or not suited to the particular needs of the moment, but always there were enough practical, applicable ideas to meet each assignment.

You would think, after this personal proof of the effectiveness of the unfettered creative method that I would naturally have followed the same method when I turned to the field of artistic expression.

But instead I struggled, strained, suffered, and produced nothing that gave me happiness or satisfaction. Why?

For years I could not answer this question. Then light began to dawn. In my art work I was inhibited by lack of self-confidence and the fear that I might be breaking rules I knew nothing about. No creative person could create hampered by such shackles. So naturally as an artist I failed completely.

A Little Child's Example

Don't imagine that during this fallow, feckless period I utterly abandoned my artistic searchings. I read every art book I could find; visited art galleries; studied great paintings and not-so-great paintings. I also tried to paint now and then, but always I produced meaningless copies of someone else's style. I went through periods of experimentation with oil, tempera, casein, and water color. The subjects of these experimental paintings were usually still lifes or Greco-like faces of ineffable sadness (the latter probably expressing my inward sorrow at my artistic failures).

Then, in disgust and frustration, I turned away from artistic experiments and didn't lift a brush or a pencil for more than fifteen years!

When a new way of life on a retirement schedule permitted a reinvestigation of art, I discovered, to my amazement, that of all the contemporary paintings examined, the only ones that pleased or intrigued me were those produced by children.

Children's art, I found, had simplicity, freedom, vitality—joy, its most priceless ingredient.

Yes, it was primitive, uncontrolled, devoid of technical skill, sometimes mystifying, but always compelling. Children's art always said something, and the heart always knew what it was saying though the intellect could not always categorize it.

I might never have found the key to the richness and the

wonder of children's art if I had not read Viktor Lowenfeld's revealing book, Your Child and His Art.

From this book I learned two things that proved of great value to me.

I learned that children's art is an expression of feeling.

Whether he is working in clay or with paint or with any other medium, the child (before he receives any directed art training) says, through his hands, how he feels about life.

The things that are important and meaningful to a child appear in a painting exaggerated in size, in placement, in coloring. And the things that are unimportant or meaningless to the child are either relegated to minor positions of placement and low-key rendition of color or disappear entirely.

Through color impact and through placement within his composition, and by means of exaggerated or diminished size, the child expresses love, hate, fear, grief, joy, the whole gamut of human emotion.

In this respect the child is not trying to reproduce the world around him but to create a reflection of the world within him.

What We May Learn From the Untrained Child Artist

The child artist, through his art, tells a story. It is a story about life and his relationship to it; about his problems, his failures, his triumphs. It is an original story, not copied from anyone else; not copied from nature, but created from the child's infinite reservoirs of feeling.

When you understand this you view children's paintings with heart-shaking awareness. Now you no longer laugh, or criticize, as some adults do, because the child's colors are chosen for love of color and for color's emotional statement rather than for their resemblance to reality.

And you suddenly realize that if adults are drawn with mile-high legs and out-of-sight heads it's because that's the way they look to a small child.

And if running horses are drawn with only flying manes and tails it is because this is the extracted essence of horse to the child, its grace and beauty encapsuled in the flick of a brush.

In expressing his feelings through his art the child finds release from tensions and frustrations; he sublimates his anxieties and his hostilities and he also pours forth his love of life. And that magic quality of joy we referred to earlier radiates in a glowing patina from the uninhibited child painting.

This, we repeat, is the expression, through art, of the UN-TRAINED CHILD ARTIST. This primitive artist allowing his feelings to take form through the medium of paint or clay or whatever, is pleasing only himself. He seeks neither fame nor fortune. He craves no one's approval.

The Influence Of Authority

But now, as Viktor Lowenfeld explains so convincingly in his book, the parent, the teacher, the figure of authority steps in and either laughs at the child's work, or criticizes it, or, perhaps more disastrously, commends it, thereby encouraging the child to do more of the same in order to win continuing approval. Or this same voice of authority demands an explanation of the art work. It must have a reason for being; it must justify its existence; it must become readily understandable to the adult mind. It must conform to adult standards of artistic "slickness"—standards set by the representational commercial art (so-called) that in most instances constitutes the only art to which the average child's parents are exposed.

Questions are asked of the child artist by the authority figure.

"Why is the man's head so small? Why are his legs so long? Why do you paint a tree yellow when trees are green? Why didn't you paint more evenly and neatly instead of slopping on your paint as you did and not keeping it within borders?"

Here we have the most poisonous question of all. And even though Viktor Lowenfeld explains with patience and passion the irrevocable damage that is done to artistic expression (in both child and adult) when the child is told to confine and contain his painting within predetermined outlines—such as those imposed in the popular children's coloring books—it wasn't until I looked back on my own childhood art experiences that I realized how pathetically wrong it is to give children coloring books with outlined figures that they are supposed to color neatly, precisely, and realistically.

The Uncontained Nonconformist

They say there are two kinds of thinking in this world: the creative and the scientific.

The scientific thinker attempts to bring order out of chaos and, through a process of logic and analysis and the painstaking assemblage of facts, arrives at conclusions which he then wants others to accept without question. This thinker establishes rules and expects others to conform to them.

The creative thinker, on the other hand, upsets the established order, frequently brings chaos out of order, but, in doing so, creates whole new areas of exploration that lead to further advances and greater progress. This thinker, through a process of intuition, with a daring and total disregard for rules, breaks out of all limitations, refuses to be contained; he denounces conformity and makes the scientific thinker fearful, uneasy, and thoroughly miserable.

Which is more important or valuable to society? Who would dare to say?

Without any doubt both are of equal importance. But unfortunately, in our present society, while the creative thinker is taught to respect the scientific thinker, the scientific thinker seldom respects the creative thinker; he denounces him for a troublemaker and either cajoles or cudgels him into conformity.

This is true especially in the field of art, where the majority of people become extremely uncomfortable if they find themselves forced to contemplate any art form that is unconventional in concept or execution and therefore not readily understandable.

Victor Lowenfeld blames the outline coloring book for much of the conformity and frustration of adult artists. And now that I realize the vast amount of psychic damage caused by the outline coloring book, I don't believe he has denounced the seemingly innocent little villain severely enough.

It took me months of patient effort to break out of the prison of self containment in which I had been jammed by the outline principle. But what joy I experienced when I at last discovered the untrammeled use of free-flowing, uncontained color!

It took me almost as long to be able to appreciate the beauty and vitality of the jagged line as opposed to the bland anonymity of whispered color and careful outlines.

Now I realize I found it so difficult to paint with any freedom because of the restrictive influence of those outline coloring books of my youth. And, since arriving at this realization, I literally shudder when I note, in a doctor's, dentist's, or optometrist's office, stacks of the offending outline coloring books offered for the imprisonment of the young. All this can lead to is another generation of conforming, frustrated artists, unless we rise up and insist that outline coloring books be replaced with plain sheets of paper and broken, messed-up crayons.

That's another point Viktor Lowenfeld makes that I agree with most heartily: As long as art materials are treated as something sacred, to be kept immaculate, stored carefully, and put away out of sight at the end of each art session, we shall never encourage our young people to enjoy the thrill of self-abandonment in art.

I'm as neat as the next person, and possibly even neater, having been raised in a home where neatness was a virtue and untidiness a cardinal sin. But I know why Viktor Lowenfeld advocates the broken crayon and the untidy paint box.

If you become so restrained that you can't throw around some paint or break a crayon or two, you'll never really let yourself go when you're caught up in an artistic endeavor.

Adults as well as children should occasionally paint as Henry Miller did during his artistic explorations at Big Sur. Artist Miller would become so obsessed by the powerful surge of artistic expression that threatened to shatter him that he would frequently sing and dance as he painted, mix colors with wild exuberance, splash paint about mightly, and howl with the sheer delight he felt at the joy of drenching himself in pure, unadulterated color.

Painting of this sort is an expression of feeling that does more for the psyche than a new mate, a new dress, or even a journey away from it all.

You may have to clean up a mess when you've finished. But that's the only time to worry about neatness, when the artistic urge subsides and you return to earth. Then, and only then, should you feel compelled to restore a semblance of order to workshop or studio.

More About Free-Flowing Creativity

So much for the wonder of children's art and the menace of the outline coloring book.

I learned much from both and will share that unfoldment with you later. For the present I'd like to mention another book that had a profound effect on me, a book that took me another step forward in understanding the difference between conformity and freedom in art expression.

The book I refer to is *On Not Being Able to Paint,* by Marion Milner, an Englishwoman, who made all sorts of fascinating discoveries in art when she set aside all rules and decided to paint in a most remarkable fashion.

Marion Milner was undergoing psychoanalysis at the time she did the painting described in her book and so she read deep psychological meaning into everything she produced, much of it over the head of the average layman, and most of it unnecessary for us to go into in our discussion.

But the important discovery Marion Milner made, which I would like to bring to your attention, is one I myself made independently, which I hape that you will explore.

She discovered that if she simply approached a blank piece of paper or canvas with paint brush or pencil in hand, without any predetermined concept of what she would produce on that paper, and simply allowed a drawing or painting to unfold without her conscious direction, she would produce all sorts of amazing, sometimes beautiful, paintings, each of which revealed deep psychological processes of thought that she had not really been aware of consciously. And these paintings not only served to release Marion Milner's tensions, anxieties, and hostilities; they also helped to clarify and eventually to solve many long-standing, deepseated emotional and personality problems.

We are not recommending that you substitute the canvas for the couch. If artistic expression resolves some of your emotional conflicts, rejoice and consider this a bonus.

What we wish to convey is the importance of following Marion Milner's method of undirected creative expression, because we believe that in doing so you will find yourself making progress that you never dreamed possible.

Art Influences Around Us

Another point must be made before we proceed to the particulars of launching you on your artistic adventure. That is the influence of the art to which you have been exposed throughout your life.

If you will stop and think for a moment, you will agree, I am sure, unless you happen to be an art connoisseur, an art teacher, a student of formal art instruction, or an artist, that the only examples of art to which you have been exposed throughout your life are: Billboard art, Magazine Illustration art, Advertising art, Television art, Department Store art. And it is questionable whether any of this "art" should be called "art" in terms of the art we discuss in this book.

Much of this art so-called, is executed (we use the word advisedly) by professional experts: commercial artists who are masters at artistic technique; persons who know all the whys and wherefores of cold versus warm colors, advancing colors versus receding colors; impact colors versus subtle colors. These skilled craftsmen know how, through clever color manipulation, to model in the round; to lead the eye through the intricacies of perspective; to develop a composition that will cause the mind to traverse a predetermined path to a focus of interest; to utilize color to produce an illusion of light and shade, closeness or distance.

But let us ask a few questions about the purpose of their "art."

These craftsmen are paid by others for their work.

They produce to please those who pay them.

They are advised not to "go beyond the heads of the public" in creating their art works.

They must, in the case of advertising art, please not only the public, but their clients.

In the case of Television Art, they must produce art that is compatible with the color complexities of the television medium, compelling to the eye but not in conflict with any products or actors who may compete with it.

In the case of magazine art, the end result must not jar the sensibilities of readers who have no knowledge of the niceties of artistic expression. It must be sufficiently "slick" to stand up well in competition with the slick advertising art that surrounds it.

The art referred to is not done to please the artist but to please his sponsor and his critics.

This art is not produced from any inner conviction but from an inner necessity to survive and to exchange one's art for the means of survival: money.

The artist produces to gain fame or fortune, not release or joy.

And since the artist produces art that will conform to the standards of the multitudes, his work will, in most cases, tend to slickness and containment.

That is the key word. Slickness. The controlled line, the emasculated or subdued color, reflect the state of the artist's psyche, his relationship to life. Everything must be brought to a state of finish or polish that leaves no room for any contribution from the beholder.

This is the type of art most of us grow up on and few of us ever manage to learn about or understand any other kind of art unless we push ourselves out of the enshackling fetters of self-containment and visit fine art galleries and museums and mingle with true artists and come to understand the principles of non-commercial art through personal experimentation.

The influence of this slick, commercial art is so deep and so broad and so overwhelming in forming your opinions of art and your reactions to art that we cannot impress upon you how important it is for you to turn away from commercialized art as you set out to find yourself as an artist.

Some Antidotes to Commercial Art

To combat the insidious influence of the commercial art that surrounds all of us today I have found some methods that may also work for you. One such method is to observe as much children's art as you possibly can.

Another is to study the works of the new, younger artists. Some of this art may puzzle you, some may even shock you, much may seem totally inexplicable to you. But look with open eyes, an open heart, and an open mind and you will soon see that these young people, if sincere, are making statements about life that could be made no other way.

In this art of the young you will see much that is daring and different. Learn to separate the different for the sake of difference from the different because of basic personality differences and you certainly find something to admire.

The sincere artist today is not afraid to experiment with every available medium. This experimentation is healthy and good for the artist as it is good for the future of art. We will have more to say on this subject later.

But we have had enough words for the present. Let's get on with the real substance of art—let's go into action.

2

The Tremulous Take-Off

Overcoming Those First-Attempt Jitters

If you're as uncertain of your art capabilities at this moment as I was when first I launched myself on my voyage of self-discovery as an artist, you have my heartfelt sympathy.

At this moment, though you may not believe it, what you need least is direction or instruction.

This is the moment to leap off the dock, take the plunge, and sink or swim on your own efforts, if you'll pardon a very badly mixed metaphor.

At the most a teacher could only encourage you and in doing so postpone—but only for a very little while—the moment when you would still have to go forward on your own steam.

And so, if you expected us to take you by the hand and lead you gently forward, we are sorry to disappoint you. Instead we are going to give you a psychic shove, with this one small shred of comfort: where you now venture, we ventured first. We went under many times, but now we find—O mirabile dictu!—we are able to do more than dog paddle.

Strike out bravely and before long, you, too, will find yourself not only in the swim and holding your own with other self-taught artists, but very likely executing some fancy artistic acrobatics.

And now, to give you that initial propulsion which each of us must have, in one form or another, if ever we hope to leave the shelter of a friendly shore, we give you a first assignment.

ASSIGNMENT NUMBER I
Take a handful of paper clips. You must have some in your

27

Paper clips presented in two ways; against a light ground, painted black and against a dark ground left unpainted (opposite). The variations are endless. Grab a handful of paper clips in various sizes and see what happens.

home; most people do. Then take a piece of dark construction paper or black loose-leaf notebook paper about eight and a half by eleven inches in size and fool around with the paper clips till you produce what appears to you to be a design.

Do you like it?

Fine. The only purpose of your assignment was to cause you to create a design that seemed pleasing to YOU.

When the final design suits you, paste the paper clips to the paper, mount the paper to a larger paper of a contrasting color, and hang it up where you can look at it now and then.

You have now expressed yourself artistically without any coercion, direction, or reaction from anyone other than yourself. This is the pattern your assignments will follow throughout the book. We hope you will do all of them. You may do them in any order that pleases you. Keep the results around till you tire of

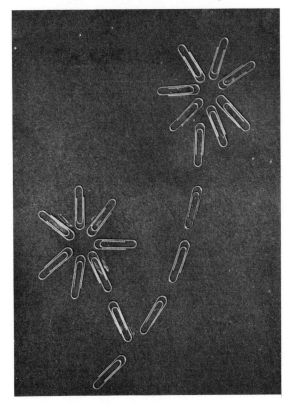

them or feel that you have grown beyond them. At that point you may retire them with the intention of later displaying them at a showing of your art. Or you may dismantle them and use the materials for other purposes. Or you may give them away as gifts. I have followed all three methods. But when I give away art works I tell the recipients I may want to borrow them later for an art show. They are always very cooperative.

We feel certain you can create at least five other designs with paper clips that will be rhythmic and appealing and that will demonstrate effectively that art *is* all around us. Why not try? And as you do, think of other ways that paper clips might be used decoratively. As necklaces, earrings, bracelets, anklets, belts, picture borders, or as Christmas tree garlands? Painted various colors? What other ways?

ASSIGNMENT NUMBER 2

Let's continue to explore the artistic possibilities of articles found in the stationery store, the office, the desk drawer.

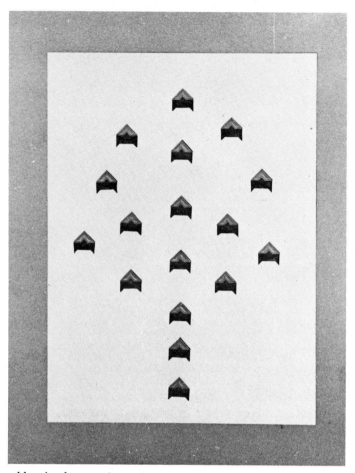

The starkly simple tree is made from the corner mounts used to anchor snapshots in family albums. The mounts are black and red against a lemon ground. The matting paper is red. If you have some picture mounts, see what other designs they suggest to you.

Take several sheets of construction paper in various colors, including black—the eight and a half by eleven-inch paper will do —and without any preconceived notions and without copying any existing design, see what designs you can develop from the following: typewriter ribbon, paper fasteners, rubber bands; felt pen caps and flashbulb holders, snapshot corner mounts and looseleaf reinforcements.

Are there any other things you could make with the articles

Design made from eleven keys painted black and glued to the front of a discarded drawer painted soft tangerine.

Twenty-six paper fasteners and two brass curtain rings form this design of interrelated pinwheels.

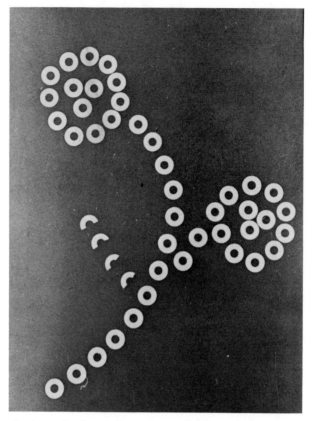

White looseleaf notebook reinforcements glued to dark green construction paper form the basis for myriad floral and geometric designs, of which this is only one happy example.

we've just talked about? Think about it and do some experimenting.

ASSIGNMENT NUMBER 3

A search in the medicine cabinet or a trip through the drug store reveals the artistic possibilities in both. This time we shall line up a box of cotton balls of the type used for removing nail polish; a tin of sheer, assorted-shape Bandaids; a few leftover hair curler pins; some plastic toothpicks; and the plastic paddle from an old, very old, biff-bat ball.

What would you make with this assortment, using construction paper not only in the eight and a half by eleven inch size, but also in the larger twelve by eighteen inch size?

Select a piece of construction paper in the color that pleases you and reach for any of the items that suggest a design in embryo.

I place my construction paper on a piece of scrap board or on cardboard so I can move it around after I place the design ingredients on it without having it flop and upset my creation.

I lay out the design tentatively first and frequently find I must arrange and rearrange, add, subtract, simplify, and sometimes redo the entire design from scratch before I am satisfied with it. The satisfaction comes from an inner sense of agreement with the final arrangement that tells me: "This is it! Don't tamper further."

Sunbursts of toothpicks flower in a design of delicate beauty.

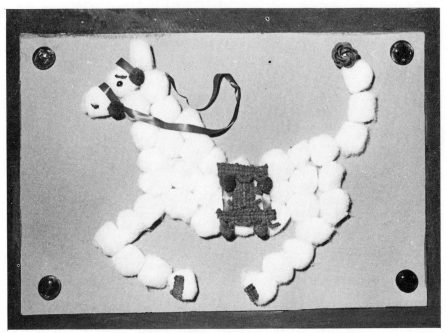

The background for this pert, prancing cotton-ball horse is a sheet of cardboard 18″ x 8″ painted dark green. A sheet of construction paper slightly smaller is glued to this background—its color a soft sage green. The four corners are decorated with emerald green gem mosaics. The halter is red leather cut from a toy bear's harness. The saddle is bright red fringe. A bright red rose adorns the tail. What other animals can you make from cotton balls? Try making some.

At no time do I strive for a particular design or a copied design but let the texture, shape, color, and movement of the selected elements dictate their own arrangement.

Almost always I find that simplification of any design and the removal of extraneous elements are what is required to make the design psychically acceptable.

I have conducted many experiments among friends, children, and even strangers, to see what designs they produce with the same elements when I ask them to create something without predetermination.

Invariably they go through three stages or display three kinds of reaction to my request.

First they are embarrassed, nonplussed, and make protestations (in the case of adults) as to their complete lack of creativity or artistic ability.

The bedazzling and beautiful tree is made from an assortment of plastic bandaids in a pale muted pink against black construction paper.

The children, unless they are disturbed or inhibited children with problems in their lives, simply reach for the elements and make something—usually something beautiful and distinctive. That is, children under eight usually do.

Older children display the same embarrassment and withdrawal shown by adults, and must be coaxed or even flattered before they relax sufficiently to attempt anything creative.

When older children or adults get past this initial embarrassed reluctance and I turn away from them, remove my attention from them, and they get the feeling that they are not being watched or directed, they too usually create an interesting and distinctive design, a fact that never fails to delight and astonish them. All the while, of course, they continue to declare their total lack of "artistic ability."

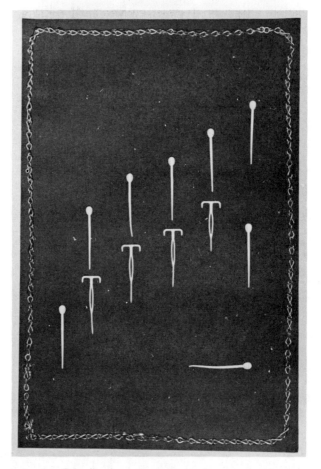

"The Organization Man" who goes down as he goes up, is executed in pink plastic hair curler pins against a black ground with a plumber's chain border.

You will find in this book many examples of such impromptu creations, with credit given in each case to the original artist who professed total lack of artistic ability.

What fascinates me, always, besides the thrill of seeing someone who has been inhibited in artistic areas or who has a deep sense of personal inferiority in these areas suddenly radiate the joy that accompanies unfettered artistic expression, is the endless variety of designs that appear from the same elements.

The Cochina Doll, above, is made from looseleaf paper markers against a dark ground.

The rabbit, evolved from an assemblage of five plastic ends from oven foil rollers. The ears are cut from white plastic picnic spoons.

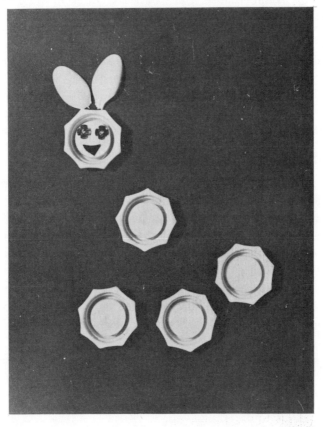

Children's picture blocks for display on dressers in a child's room or nursery are made by pasting cut-outs from Christmas cards to wood scraps and painting the wood blocks a different color on each exposed side, ranging from blue, green, and violet through red, orange, pink, and yellow, all in hot vivid tones. Then spray paint with clear plastic spray to render waterproof. Be sure these are kept where a child can't handle them or put them in his mouth unless you use special non-toxic paints for your decoration.

No two persons in the world, it seems, will ever produce exactly the same design if left undirected, just as no two persons will write identically or share the same verbal mannerisms.

But in almost all instances each design, though differing from all others, will contain elements of beauty and orderliness—unless, of course, the personality of the designer is seriously disturbed. The personality damage will always appear in the design as disorder, incompleteness, or even as absolute chaos—this usually with the very young.

And invariably the withdrawn, inhibited personality will produce designs of contraction and withdrawal whereas the outgoing, exuberant individual will produce designs that reflect ebullience and buoyancy.

If you wish to preserve your designs for later reference and

Biff Bat Cat made from an old biff bat toy. The mane is black fringe, the eyes and nose of felt, the bow bright orange.

comparison, or simply out of affection for them, do as I do and anchor them in place with Wilhold Glue when you feel completely satisfied with them.

I've learned a few secrets of applying the glue successfully, which I'll gladly share with you, realizing that you may make even more wonderful discoveries on your own. In gluing very fine pieces such as toothpicks or paper clips and in gluing lengthy strips such as pieces of string, rickrack, or yarn, I've found it easier to transfer the glue from a large container to a plastic squeeze bottle with a conical tip.

Place a slender nail or a curtain pin in the open end of the conical top of this plastic squeeze bottle and remove the nail or

"Wheels Within Wheels" is made from any discarded wheel-like metal scrap I could find at the junk yard. The background is black, the wheels painted orange, pink, red, yellow, and lime green. A brilliant gem mosaic flashes at the center of each wheel. Note the unusual hanging made by tacking a rugged piece of black leather to the top of the board with heavy duty tacks.

pin only while you're using the glue, replacing it each time between pourings. In this way the glue is always available, comes out in a thick or thin stream, depending on the angle at which you tilt the bottle and the size of the opening. For the items I mentioned above, I apply the glue to the surface I am decorating in fine lines first and then lay the toothpicks or the paper clips or the string or whatever along the line of glue, pressing them down with a fingernail after they are in place.

This seems to work much better than applying the glue to the article and then pressing the article to the surface you wish to decorate. Try it and see if you don't agree.

And while we're on the subject of glue, I find Wilhold satisfactory for every decorative purpose because it dries clear and

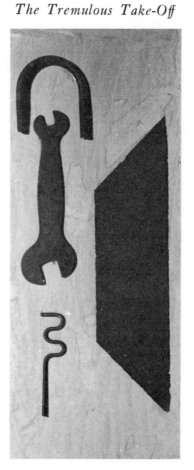

"Necktie Party" is made from a motley collection of hardware painted black and glued to a background board painted shocking pink.

The almost-Grecian frieze above was made by gluing curtain pins painted white to a strip of molding painted midnight blue.

Wishbones painted white and glued to a wood scrap, spray painted a rich flat black, form this spidery, delicate design. A piece of narrow white piping with a fluted edge trails among the wishbones, emphasizing the rhythmic grace of the design.

invisible, washes off fingers and other surfaces easily, and provides a bond when thoroughly dry (usually a matter of twenty-four to forty-eight hours) that will hold anything to anything—at least this has been my experience.

Since I am not a seamstress and I am an impatient craftsman not given to the creation of time-consuming delicate effects, I make two thirds of my things through the stick-together method and use glue by the gallon.

In working with glue this intensively I've found that it is not only a clean, dependable, and cooperative adhesive but a versatile craft tool with artistic possibilities of its own.

For instance, I've discovered that you can pour glue directly from the bottle (with conical tip removed) onto a wooden surface and create all sorts of free-form designs. If you mix a little cornstarch with the glue it will acquire even more body and you can create interesting bas-relief or raised effects. By allowing the glue to pour from the bottle as you twist and turn it in curlycues or whirls you can make fascinating picture frames.

When the glue dries (and you will have to allow extra drying time for glue of this consistency applied in depth) you can spray it or hand paint it with any kind of paint, or gild it or flock it or just give it a clear plastic finish. Later it may be antiqued if you wish, and in the case of picture frames it will acquire a permanent, gesso-like finish.

Some Asides on the Collection of Art Materials

The experimenting, exploring artist wants to investigate every medium, every material, every creative possibility offered by man and by nature, and this is exactly as it should be.

Decorative builder's grille board sprayed gold, edged in purple, and glued together in the shape of a cross makes a beautiful wall hanging (hang with a piece of gold plumber's chain.) The center ornament is a gold foil gift wrap emblem edged in Radiant Tempera to match the cross border.

Textures, rough and smooth, will intrigue you—textures of wood, of fabric, of paint.

The physical excitement of color will astonish you. But we'll go into the whole stimulating subject of color later.

Patterns will delight you.

Lines will entice you.

Wood, leather, metal, cloth, plastics, everything you see and touch will open up new vistas for you. Each of these artistic stimulants will reveal a new facet of your artistic capabilities that you never knew existed.

Naturally, unless you have unlimited sums of money at your disposal you won't be able to afford all the arts and crafts materials that you will suddenly crave. But don't let this dishearten you. No artist can ever afford all the materials he yearns to pos-

Spoons rescued from an incinerator but badly charred were contributed by Sharon Moss. I gave them the appearance of antiqued copper by painting them with haphazard streakings of first blue, then green Radiant Tempera and painted bright little floral designs in their centers in hot tones of orange, pink, and yellow. Glued to a board painted a deep blue-green with a French blue border, they made a handsome wall ornament.

sess and the yearning is part of the excitement that leads to artistic inventiveness.

There are sources of materials that you will eventually become aware of and that you will enjoy making use of, and I will now attempt to reveal these little-known, abundant sources of art supplies.

Thrift stores and junk piles, friends' and merchants' cast-offs —these provide the hidden manna that will help to make you an artist.

As soon as friends realize that you are serious about your art

A wood scrap stained walnut and bordered in black provides a backdrop for the Indian Pony made from horseshoe nails. The hanging at the top of the board is made from heavy black leather in keeping with the rugged character of the plaque.

expression and that you are looking for art in everything around you, you will be thrilled to discover that they will derive personal satisfaction from supplying you with items that will test your ingenuity and encourage your creativity.

Ever since I began my own artistic experiments, friends have joyously contributed old spools, yarn collections, Christmas cards, broken jewelry, gift-wrap papers, and things I couldn't possibly enumerate because the supply has been endless.

In addition I soon discovered that many merchants are just as eager to become a budding artist's sponsor. I have a friend, George Mockry, who is an upholsterer, and he has supplied me with fabric swatches and samples from which I have made wall hangings, abstract paintings, picture frames, place mats, hot dish pads—all sorts of things.

A man who runs a carpet shop has made similar contributions.

A plumber saves old copper toilet floats, from which other remarkable "works of art" have been fashioned.

Bowling pins discarded by a bowling alley were introduced into my life by a young friend, Robbin Day, who turns them into book ends and whimsical figurines.

Another friend, who runs an ice cream route, searches in trash cans along his route and brings me old restaurant candle holders, picture frames in need of mending, and advertising displays that can be turned into quite tasteful bric-a-brac with a little imagination.

But the greatest wealth has been unearthed at a local cabinet shop. Here I have found wood scraps, doors, drawers, molding, pressed wood, plywood, veneers, in fact wood of every size, shape, and description, from which I have made wall ornaments, toys, figurines, nursery plaques, paintings, frames—fully a third of the articles pictured in this book.

So if there is a cabinet shop anywhere near you, I hope you will investigate its cast-off materials in search of artistic inspiration. You will first have to explain your desires to the owner or manager and get permission to look in the bins where waste materials are

"Walking over the Waves" executed in tangled wire on rusted tin. The movement, beauty, and delicacy captured in this photograph by Arnold Wall show how even the lowliest sources may provide an object of beauty that stabs at the heart.
Created by Carol Boynton

What more unique as a nursery wall plaque than a baby carry-all with an angel at its base made from an Ivory Liquid Detergent bottle? The color scheme is white, blue, gold, and lavender with artificial lilacs to add a special touch.

tossed before the bins are emptied by the local trash collector.

I have worked out a plan for doing this that causes the least inconvenience to the shop owner, trying always to arrive when the workers are on a lunch break and things are quiet in the yard.

I visit the shop twice a week at a specified agreed-upon time and always find something new and wonderful, since the work within the shop varies from time to time and you never know what treasure will turn up.

The freedom of painting on wood at no cost was what really permitted me to explore every kind of painting medium until I began to turn out paintings that others thought enough of to want to buy them.

I've never painted on anything but cast-off materials; I've never worked with any frames but those I created, and the results must be satisfactory since the paintings are selling.

This perky piglet candleholder made itself. It is a vertebra from a steer. I simply painted it here and there with pink and black paint to accentuate its outlines, glued on a black curtain ring, and then pasted a white candle in place. It has been one of the sensations of the art studio—conclusive proof that art is where you find it. (Vertebra contributed by Carol Boynton.)

Is there beauty in an old, beat-up toilet float? There is in this one with its assemblage of unnameable hardware. Mounted on a seasoned, heavily-grained board and antiqued with blue and green tempera to resemble ancient copper, it has become a paper weight elegant enough to grace the finest desk.

We'll talk more about this matter of materials later. Right now, a little assignment.

ASSIGNMENT NUMBER 4

Using whatever scrap wood you can lay hands on and any paint you may come across, whether it happens to be tempera, oil, old house paint, lipstick, nail polish, or food coloring mixed with cornstarch—make some free-form paintings of whatever comes to mind and see what you bring forth.

It isn't necessary to prime your wood, though you may spray it with a white undercoating if you wish. I prefer to let the graining of the wood reveal itself in the final painting and I like the wood tone better than a cold primer as a background for my paintings because they seem to acquire more warmth and interest this way.

What will you paint? It doesn't matter in this world what evolves—a flower, a tree, an animal, a child, a house, or just delightful color patterns. The point is that what appears must not be predetermined; it must not be copied from another Painting or a real-life object; it must come out of you.

We Draw or Paint Best What We Like Best

Study the works of any artist and you will soon discover that certain objects continually reappear in that artist's paintings, as do certain colors.

Picasso is famous for his man-woman figures, Cezanne for his riotous colors. Artists go through blue periods and pink periods. Some draw roosters best, others lean toward geometrics, others cling to whispery colors, whimsy, or romanticism.

What have we here? A very old board. A slice of native agate polished by a friend at a local rock club (upper left). A piece of cactus skeleton and two black iron hinges and (center bottom) a piece of leather antiqued a rich orange-brown.

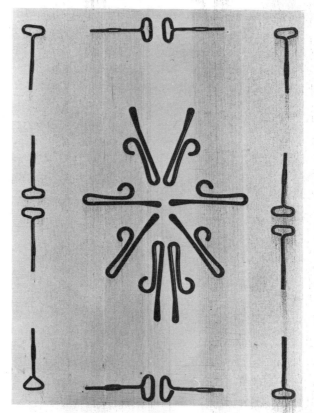

If there is anything less likely to inspire art in the beholder it's the black plastic stretchers on which men's socks are hung. But see what happens when the same stretchers are teamed up with a border of keys from anchovy cans. Could you find a more satisfying or distinctive design?

At first you'll wonder what in the world to paint. And more frequently than not, whatever you do produce will appear embarrassingly distasteful to you. In fact, you may utterly loathe it.

Please persist till you get past this period.

You are forcing when this happens and not letting a painting unfold from within without prompting or coercion.

Throw away the things that really upset you so they won't haunt or discourage you. But don't throw them too far away. Later you may like them or somebody else will. The first time this happened to me and someone raved over an effort I'd gladly have buried, I was disturbed and puzzled. Was it possible that I didn't even know what was good or bad in my work? This possibility can really unnerve you.

Now I've learned not to let anything about my painting upset me—my own reactions to it or anyone else's. People are always going to read into your painting something that you didn't see there. This is fine. Let them. They are making a contribution when they do this and the contribution endears the work to them far more than anything you might contribute. And their contribution may be what makes them wish to own your creation.

I'm ashamed to tell you how long it took me to arrive at this realization. But the happy letting go was the first step toward an increase in self-confidence.

I found, too, that there are certain things I like to paint or draw and if I will let myself do these things, no matter how many I may produce of a similar character, they will be my better efforts.

And no two will ever be identical since each will reflect my emotional state or my mental viewpoint at the time of creation, and no two emotional or mental states will be identical.

I am happiest and seem to have the happiest results when I paint horses that I have known and loved all my life; fish, since they have a design that pleases me; flowers, because I am mad for them; trees, which I worship; and slightly whimsical compositions with perhaps a surprise element here and there or a little barb of commentary on contemporary life.

Of course, if you were to add all these things up you'd find me. The purpose of your painting must be to find you.

Variation On A Theme

In finding yourself you will travel down a path this is neither straight nor direct. Many times it will double back upon itself, becoming involved in seemingly meaningless convolutions; sometimes it will come to a halt in a cul-de-sac or even in a dry and apparently profitless wasteland.

But however devious this path of self-discovery you will eventually learn that nothing is wasted along the way, nothing is fragmented; all is part of the main; your total personality is disclosing itself.

And so you will repeat many designs, choose repeatedly similar subjects to dwell upon. Leaping horses or tenuous flowers will appear and reappear in different arrangements, wearing different colors.

You are turning the gem to the light, as they say in advertising, when this happens. You are playing variations on a theme. You are having secret, silent fun. But you are not in a rut. You do not lack creative imagination. Enjoy your variations. Ponder them. Some you'll like better than others. Each will express a different mood and reveal a different phase of your artistic development.

About Cherished Imperfections

And now a word about your less than perfect creations. The untrained artist does not produce work with the slickness, the polish, the (apparent) perfection of the trained commercial artist. We touched on this matter of slickness versus improvisation before but we wish to elaborate on the subject because it is so important for you to understand it.

Chances are, if you were raised in America in an average middle-class or lower-than-middle-class home, you have been exposed to commercial art or mass produced "factory" art most of your life.

Repeatedly we must caution you not to allow this pseudo-art to set any standards for your work.

Imperfections account for much of the charm of primitive art. The slickness and polish of commercial art account for much of its dullness.

I couldn't draw a straight border if I tried and I don't try. The quaver in my borders I consider my trademark.

Mistakes happen. When they do, instead of giving way to despair or redoing your work, capitalize on the mistake; encourage it to become something magnificent in its own right. You'll be astonished to discover that the most splendid results grow out of artistic mishaps.

And the Glory of Color

We cannot talk impersonally or dispassionately about something we love. This is why I can only talk personally and with passion about color, which I have grown to love madly.

This was not always so and I believe I know why.

Color is and always will be and always should be an intensely personal matter. You and you alone can decide what colors please you—and, conversely, what colors do not please you. Because

The ferocious but lovable Tiki God is made from brown wax cast in a plastic mold. The background is driftwood and dried grass. The accent colors are orange, pink, and yellow.

color is inextricably part of your emotions. And so color will always be related to feeling.

The colors you like are liked because they are associated (consciously or unconsciously) with pleasant experiences in your life. And the colors you dislike are disliked because they are associated (consciously or unconsciously) with unpleasant experiences in your life.

In this simple and primitive manner you can determine your color palette. Choose the colors that cause you to feel deeply. Notice I didn't say choose the colors you like; the colors that give you a lift—unless you wish to express euphoric feelings or paint

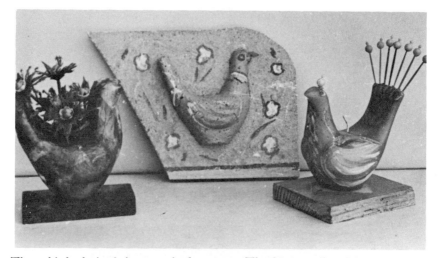

Three birds derived from a single source. The bird on the right is of wax cast in a plastic mold, painted in vibrant orange and pink, with tail made of brightly colored toothpicks and pop beads. The center bird is in bas relief made from half of the same mold, cast this time in papier mâché, colored pink, violet, and yellow and glued to a pressed wood scrap painted orange. The bird on the left is the original mold covered with pink and purple tissue paper cut in thin strips and glued in place haphazardly. The center of the mold is filled with bright blue and red plastic flowers. Bases are scraps of wood stained with walnut stain.

happy pictures. You may want to do this. I find that in most instances I do.

But the point we wish to make is that you must choose colors that move you, whether they express your happy feelings or your sad feelings. As long as they stir you, release your emotions, and make a loud and clear statement—those are the colors to work with.

Your happy-association colors will be your outgoing, uplifting colors. But your unhappy-association colors may very well express your deeper, more secret, shy and subtle feelings. Your mood at the moment of creation will determine which colors to work with.

Color Theories, Color Rules

Back in the arid, agonizing days when I wanted so much to become an accepted conventional, I-know-the-rules artist I tried very hard to understand color rules and color theories. Tried but never made it.

I studied the color wheel. I read the most profound books on the physics and the chemistry of color.

I tried to keep the primaries and the secondaries and the tertiaries in their place.

I memorized the warms and the cools, the complementaries, and the hues and the tones and the shades and the advancing and the receding colors.

I became quite expert at knowing which were which and being able to mix and match, dilute and intensify. All to no purpose. This technical knowledge of color did nothing for my painting. All it did was make me timid, fearful, constrained, self-conscious, a worrisome copyist.

I looked at some old painting tries from many years ago recently and I was so astonished at their drabness, their stiffness, their correctness—from a color sense—that I did away with them.

My colors of that period were either precise and carefully related or circumspectly and genteelly muted.

Design made from bread wrapper fastenings glued to a background of construction paper. How many other designs can you create with bread wrapper fastenings?

Color in the Raw

Now let me tell you something about my colors of today, some examples of which may be seen in this book. They are raw, wild, unrelated, psychedelic, if you insist, but I refuse to associate the word with my colors because it has been so abused, misused, and has so many sick and sorry, totally inaccurate connotations.

Today my colors sing, soar, swing, surge, shout, laugh, get angry; poke fun at the world; refuse to conform; and I do all these things with them.

I don't care if they are warm, cool, advancing, receding, compatible with other colors, brash, bold, or outspoken. If I like them; if they please me, I use them.

What caused this metamorphosis?

As recently as a few months ago I couldn't have answered that question but I believe that now I can because the answer has revealed itself to me.

I have changed so completely as a person that the change in my personality is reflected in my changed color palette.

For many years, as I have mentioned previously, I worked at a career which, while it was successful and remunerative, was not emotionally satisfying. I remained in advertising because it was a lucrative field.

Also, because I enjoy writing and having ideas, I found the work interesting. I also found it psychically corrosive. The politics became increasingly distasteful. And always, I had to write to please totally noncreative people who really had no understanding of the creative process—no realization of the tender nurturing required to bring creativity to fruition.

I conformed to the requirements of my profession, its taboos and its shibboleths. For years I wore my hair as I was expected to; dressed with (alleged) smartness and restraint; said the right things at the right time to the right people; and reaped my just rewards: promotions; salary increases; permission to keep on conforming.

It was three years after retiring from advertising before I could even begin to break the habits of conformity!

I found I was still acting, dressing, talking like an advertising woman. But less and less frequently was I thinking like one.

The great revelation came when I suddenly discovered I did not have to please anyone but myself! I could dress as I pleased, wear my hair as I pleased, do as I pleased—even paint as I pleased.

It was at this point that I began experimenting with color.

At this same point in time—most fortuitously—I became acquainted with Radiant Tempera—the luminous paints (which I will not call psychedelic though others do) that "sock-it-to-you" in the color department.

These colors have a physical and psychical impact that is liberating. They are the colors that soar, sing, twang, swing, and I began to fly with them to new heights of released creativity.

I found that I actually loved these raw, untamed colors.

(Of course they've been no secret to the Mexicans for centuries, which perhaps explains why I have always loved Mexican art—for its unstudied, unrestrained primitive quality.)

The hot pinks, the vibrant oranges, the singing yellows opened up a world of warmth and sunniness that seemed to be the world I'd always been seeking.

This color sings the song I sing in my innermost heart.

This is the way I really feel about life. Bursting with joy.

Through the medium of these colors (and I'll have more to say about them later when we go deeper into materials and methods), I found that I was able to communicate, to make statements about life and living that others could hear and respond to.

Color Changes Are More Than Surface Changes

You won't have the same experience with color that I had. You are you and your relationship to color and your use of it must reflect you. Maybe you will want to tiptoe through the quiet colors and whisper a message so gentle, so tender, that others must bend close in order to hear it.

All well and good. We are simply stating our experience in the hope that it will help you, encourage you to find yourself through your color choices.

Every color is wonderful and says something wonderful. Let it speak for you; let it say what you have to say.

Forget the theories. Ignore the rules. Dismiss the technicalities. But have fun with color. Explore. Experiment. Without fear. Without shyness. Then let the wonder and beauty and the dynamics of color illumine your whole life.

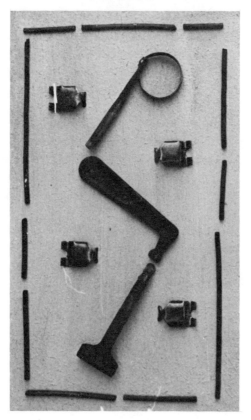

Proving once again that art is where the eye beholds it. This design in black against a green ground is composed of a discarded razor, two unidentifiable metal scraps, and a frame of artist's charcoal.

Nature knows no wrong colors; no unsuitable colors; no incompatible colors—nor should you. All color theories, all color rules, were invented by people and may be broken. Remember this. The color combination that pleases you, that satisfies you, that says what you are FEELING is the right color combination for you.

Color Fads, Fancies, Foibles

As you develop your color sense and become freer in your use of color you'll soon realize that colors have fads. This has been true down the centuries and of course is just as apparent today as it has been in the past.

In an age when most people are trying to please other people, out of fear or hope of reward, it is difficult to remain completely honest in one's choice of color.

The tastemakers will always try to influence your color selection by making speeches and writing articles about which colors are in, which colors are out, which colors are acceptable, and which colors are gauche.

The tastemakers, as you know, are the public relations and publicity people; the television art directors and producers; the interior decorators and fashion designers; the dilettantes and the art connoisseurs; the oppressive opinionated art critics. These loud and divergent voices try very hard to outshout each other and really the only ones listening are the merchants who hope in some piteous way to develop wares that will please the whole pack of taste arbiters—an impossible task.

You have set out to develop your own taste, define your own artistic expression, conform to your own standards, and decide what colors you like to work with.

So if one year the blue-greens are "fashionable" and the next year the hot pinks are de rigueur, you ignore both the blue greens and the hot pinks unless you happen to like them and find that they make statements that you want to make.

Do you like to italicize certain elements of your painting by outlining areas in black, jagged outlines? Then tear in there with your compelling, shattering black and be damned to those who say the uncouth black vulgarizes your art!

Be bold. Be brash. But above all be yourself in your choice of color, and I hope you'll have the same experience I had. When I began to abandon the conventional whispery colors and let myself go in a riot of clashing, vital, my-choice colors my paintings began to sell. And do you know what people said they liked about them—what made them lay out good cash for them—what made them rave over them and delight in them? Not their sensitivity or their artistry or their finesse or their refinement or their correctness; these things they totally lacked. People began to buy my paintings, they said, because the couldn't resist their "grabbing" colors.

And so, innocently, all unknowingly, I discovered a secret: What you lack in technique you can make up in color. Soaring, singing, swinging color covers a multitude of sins, both of omission and commission. Try being colorful, as a person and as an artist, and you will sell your paintings, too.

A Few Comments on Abstract Art

"Is it a bird? Is it a man? Is it a mystery?"

Paintings that raise questions of this sort are usually abstract paintings and they will be defended stridently or derided raucously, depending on whether the "ins" or the "outs" happen to be viewing them.

For those of you who are trying to free yourselves from the shackles of timidity and conventionalism we recommend experimentation with abstract painting. This uninhibited expression of form and color can be very helpful to you.

A painting doesn't have to "be" anything to achieve its purpose: expression of feeling that establishes communication between two minds. The feeling may be expressed in line, form, color, mass, but the end result need not resemble any recognizable object.

In the book "Abstract Art," which we believe every non-artist should ponder, Frederick Gore makes this statement:

"It is often said that the camera has forced painters to eliminate description from their work. The causes of the revolution (in art) lie deeper: it is against that mechanistic view of the universe and that faith in material things which is the background of the camera and of popular demand for an art which is wholly imitative. The artist must seek reality beneath the surface. His function becomes prophetic. For when philosopher and physicist, psychologist and sociologist, each withdraws into his own small rock of specialized certainties, only the painter and the poet may explore the unknown area between." (Page 14)

The untrained (and therefore unfettered) artist will frequently do his best in the field of abstract art. Here there is no need to paint landscapes, seascapes, "mug-scapes," or still lifes. Simply take up your brush and paint poetry; paint the color of wind and the rhythm of music; the glory of galaxies and the lift of weightlessness; paint the sound of tears and the deeps of laughter; paint the force of rage and the pale tones of tenderness.

Don't direct; don't control. Let it happen.

ASSIGNMENT NUMBER 5

Take several wood scraps of any size or shape or thickness, of pressed wood or plywood; or take some cardboard, or any paper that pleases you, and, using any old brushes that happen to be handy in a size that appeals to you, splash some colors on your background.

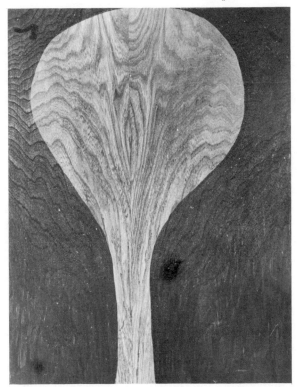

The atomic free form design above evolved from the natural wood grain on this plywood fragment. The surrounding background has been stained black. The hanging is unusual and consists of a piece of ¼" leather tied through two holes made in the board and extending to a foot-long loop by which the picture is hung. The knotted ends of the leather are visible above the central design.

Don't decide in advance what you want to paint. Don't decide in advance what colors you will use.

Here are some choices of paints to use. (I always use whatever is in current supply.) You could use powdered tempera, which you mix with water yourself to any desired consistency. (I like it thick to give texture.)

Or you could use show card tempera. Or Radiant Tempera (the hot psychedelic temperas available at stationery and paint stores).

Or household enamel, or any leftover paints that happen to be piling up in the garage.

I don't recommend that you use watercolor, which requires either more skill or more boldness than may be yours at the moment. And I keep away from oils for fun painting because they have an aura of seriousness about them that frequently hampers a beginning artist. Also they cost more than the water or casein base paints and they're messier to clean up after and require special thinners and take a long time to dry, all factors that tend to get in the way of the sort of carefree abandon we're asking you to express at the moment.

When I do use oils I don't use them in any way approved by any conventional artist. I poke my brush directly in the tube or squeeze the oil directly on the surface I'm painting on and I never use any thinner but kerosene or cheap paint thinner and my brushes are an unholy "jabbled" (made-up word) mess, but their unholiness produces all sorts of unexpected and exciting results.

But back to the temperas (or caseins, which are milk base paints quite acceptable for the present assignment because they dry quickly and require only water for a medium.) I never mix my colors to blend them into other than original shades unless they happen to mix themselves on the canvas (fancy name for work surface, whatever it may be). I find pre-mixing, especially of the Radiant Temperas, dilutes their brilliance, tones down their exuberance, and takes away the raw vital shock of color that twangs like heartstrings when you allow it to remain pure and undefiled.

But do swish your brush in clear water between changes of color, to keep colors clean and clear. And keep your water fairly clean.

A splash of sea-green Whip-Wax against a black ground results in the action painting "Waves Dancing."

CREATIVITY," made by dropping a blob of brown paint, a blob of range paint, and a blob of red paint on a moist yellow background. The titude of the "monster" toward the flower is the attitude of the average nformist toward creative expression.

"The Snake Bit," a whimsy made by painting the snake and tree on an oval paper platter and outlining the edge with green rickrack. The fruit was made by casting plaster in plastic half molds. The plaster was then tinted with tempera colors and the Della Robbia figures were glued to the platter.

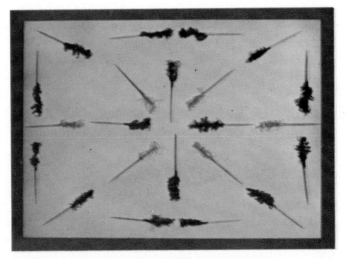

The little fuzzy "pantlets" used to decorate lamb chops or to anchor sandwiches appear in this collage as a decorative design.

The Chess Queen is made of wax cast in a half mold, painted sage green, then glued to a wood scrap painted in brilliant Radiant Red Tempera. Broken glass forms a pseudo-frame.

Design executed on the antiqued wood segment of a redwood tub formerly used for landscape gardening. The design elements are two TV capacitors gleaned from our broken-down TV set and some odd bits of broken crockery found on a hillside hike.

"Surf's Up!" was made by splashing blue tempera paint on a board used to carry mortar, already splotched with white from long use in cement mixing.

he top of an oil drum contributed by our local Mobil Manager, Rex
reer, becomes a handsome wall plaque or serving tray when decorated
ith pieces of brilliantly colored Madras Tissue paper and glazed with a
otective overcoating of clear waterproof plastic.

An antique oval frame cast on the scrap heap was reclaimed to make this
sequin and rickrack collage glued to burlap.

Did you guess that the flower cups on this collage were the tops from felt
pens and that the base ornament is made from a collection of former flashbulb holders?

The lovely sea urchin here displayed as a wall plaque mounted on pressed
wood is made from over two hundred multi-colored plastic toothpicks.

"Twiggy," created by a young teen-age visitor, Sharon Day, is made of pipe cleaners, a styrofoam egg, colored plastic tape. Her hair is shreds of radar tracking foil dropped by a plane one day. Her bows are twists of the cellophane that enwraps hard candies. Her feet are macaroni bows, her nose and eyes and mouth, sequins. The base is a wood scrap painted raging orange, with green leaves attached.

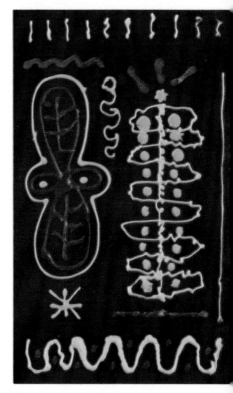

Here you see Whip-Wax, the delightful snow-white liquid plastic that yc beat to thick creaminess and then squeeze through a pastry toot to make wov pow wall plaques for nursery or den. We divided up the Whip-Wax an added food coloring to obtain the desired electrifying impact of color.

Glamorized deer antlers become a gracious addition to powder room or bath when gilded and mounted on a wood base painted a gleaming ebony. The "candle" is a curl of beeswax with plastic flowers twined about it. The delicate blown eggs and the gold spun ornament were contributed and created by Winnie Petty of Agoura, California.

Now your assignment is to just reach for whatever color says "Try me!" and apply it in any pattern that pleases you and let something unfold from the depths of you. When the work surface is decorated to your satisfaction, STOP! Always underpaint. Never overpaint. You'd only be improving on perfection, an impossibility.

When you finish this assignment hang the results around where you can look at them for further delight and encouragement. What did you produce? A flower? A tree? An animal? An abstract or a geometric design? No matter. The point of the whole assignment was to give you enjoyment and to produce something that pleased you. Keep at it till you achieve this happy result.

No Plot, No Plan

As you've probably noticed, there is no plot, no plan, no rhyme or reason to this book. It is simply telling of an art experience I want to share with you in the hope you may have a like experience. I'm telling it just as it happened and jotting down things I hope may be of help to you just as they come to mind.

So here are a few things I think we should cover, all in the interest of greater freedom and happier results.

We've all been exposed to so much of the pseudo-art referred to earlier that we must be very careful, in developing our own standards, to overcome its pernicious influence. To do this you must train yourself to avoid prettiness, sentimentality, photographic exactness, triteness, and the conventional or banal approach.

That paragraph is so important and so full of advice that you really should go back to it often and check your work against it and develop an attitude of thought that will eventually rule these destructive influences out of your life.

We'll repeat the caution because we want it to sink in and we hope you will engrave it on your memory: Avoid pretiness, sentimentality, photographic exactness, triteness, and the conventional or banal approach.

This will not be easy. Since childhood, in department stores, variety stores, restaurants, on billboards, in magazines, etc., etc., etc., you've seen the pretty pink-cheeked gamin; the vapid feathered angel; the landscape reproduced in every glaring detail of white-capped wave and waxen leaf.

Churches are white and tall spired; mothers' expressions are

A slab of native limestone found on a nature hike, about 12″ x 15″ and less than ½″ thick, shaded to creaminess at the edges from long exposure to the elements, provided an arresting background for this "prehistoric" cave drawing made with a few quick strokes of a brown felt pen. If you can find some shale or other thin rock, try your hand at this type of prehistoric drawing. You'll be amazed at what fun it is. Don't think first; just draw freely and quickly and see what emerges.

serene and noble; wives are all young, size 22-22-22, and with fine arched noses and full-blown lips. Little chicks are downy; little colts are gangly; fruit is unblemished; sidewalks are spotless.

The cult of the cute is worshiped by young and old.

Outlines of houses, people, foilage are firm and sure.
Nothing is left to the imagination. Colors are "true" and "real."

You must unlearn and unload all of this.

You must avoid prettiness, sentimentality, photographic exactness, triteness, and the conventional or banal approach.

Do you think you can?

Well, I'll tell you quite frankly I can't. I've been steeped in it too long and it creeps out in spite of my best intentions and it will in spite of yours.

But please keep trying, as I am, to grow beyond pseudo-art. It's the only way in the world to become a happy, liberated, I-don't-care-what-you-think-of-me artist.

On Being Framed

Should a painting have a frame? Or, to put the question another way, does a painting require a frame?

A hundred different artists will give a hundred different answers to these highly provocative queries.

I can only answer the questions as I found answers.

Some paintings are improved by the addition of a frame; others are not.

But a frame is not an absolute necessity.

What sort of frame should you choose?

This is one question I cannot answer for you nor would I want to, because it is so important for you to find the answer yourself.

I went to an Art Show recently to see how pictures are being framed at present. It was supposed to be a very sophisticated art show in a very sophisticated location, therefore I was shocked to see that the frames were all practically identical: white and gold or grayed down commercially made frames, to which the artist had made no contribution except possibly a few daubs of paint.

To digress from the subject of frames for a moment, it also came as a shock to note that the paintings dealt almost entirely with the same themes: landscapes; seascapes; fruit or flower still lifes, and what I call "mug-scapes"—photographic reproductions of faces.

To be certain that this wasn't just an exceptionally "square" show and possibly unique, I went to several other art shows—I refer now to open-air art shows, the kind so popular today, and not to gallery exhibits—and neither the frames nor the subject matter varied perceptibly from show to show.

Now I noticed that the age of the artists at these shows averaged from twenty-five years to fifty years.

So next I made it a point to visit some open-air shows being staged by young artists, under twenty-five.

At these shows the subject matter was far more varied and the execution of the paintings far less conventional. There were many abstracts and free-form paintings, and the few landscapes, seascapes, still lifes and "mug-scapes" were not representational; that is, they were not reproduced with the photographic exactness you are being asked to avoid.

In each case the artist made a personal contribution by means of imagination and originality. Colors were not realistic. Com-

positions did not lead the eye to the focal point of interest; perspective and dimension were often lacking. In fact, many cherished
art rules had been disregarded.

And what about frames? There were very few and the few
there were had been made by the artist and were therefore an
extension of the mood of the painting.

Needless to say, the paintings at these younger people's shows
were compelling, exciting, vibrant with life, and you could not
view them in a detached sort of way but found yourself involved
with them in spite of yourself.

And the paintings without frames seemed as complete and as
satisfying—frequently more so—than paintings with elaborate
commercial frames.

If You Must Frame

When first I started to paint, frames seemed very important
to me and a painting unfinished without one. I wanted a frame
that would lend a professional air to my painting; a frame that
would give it status and stature; a frame that would be impressive
and costly looking.

I realize now that the frame is a symbol.

It is a symbol of things far deeper than many of us ever
realize or, having realized, care to acknowledge.

The frame is a symbol of conformity; of containment; of
inhibition and restraint. The frame is a symbol of the desire for
approval—and more on this later, too.

The whole aim of this book is to set the artist within you free.
To liberate your self-expressive urges, so long controlled and
dammed up by a feeling of inadequacy and lack of confidence.

You will know you are achieving at least a portion of this
release and self-liberation when the frame of your painting seems
relatively unimportant to you.

Now don't misunderstand what we have said about frames.
We are not saying you should do without them or that you should
become self-conscious about the use of them.

We are saying this: Learn to enjoy paintings without frames.
If the painting pleases you or satisfies you without a frame then
no frame is necessary.

But, if it would please you to frame a painting and give you
a greater sense of personal satisfaction, if you feel the statement

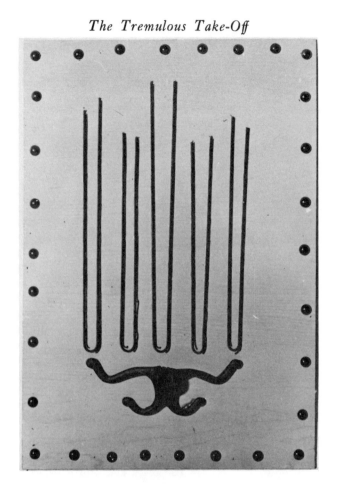

The background of the delicate candelabra is a wood scrap painted pale green. The border is made from decorative bronze upholstery tacks painted black. The base of the candelabra is two coat hangers painted black. The graceful fronds of the candelabra itself are formed of florist wire also painted black.

that the painting is making is not made without a frame, then by all means frame it!

However, in the interests of your budding creativity, do this. Make your own frame if you possibly can. By that we do not mean that you should get a mitre box, buy expensive molding, and try painstakingly to copy professional frames. Far from it.

Invent a frame for your painting that suits it; that carries its statement to completion; that causes you to feel happy with the end result. And be sure the frame is imaginative and original. Don't let the creativity of any painting stop within the borders of a conventional unimaginative frame.

The beautiful Madonna is copper foil cut from a Christmas card mounted on a discarded door painted brown in the center, black in the frame portion. The figures on the copper foil are also black and brown, which determined the color scheme, a color combination most popular at this particular moment.

With me it has been a matter of money. I simply cannot afford to buy costly frames or, in fact, any kind of frames for the endless number of paintings I now feel impelled to paint. And so, out of necessity I was forced to create my own framing devices. And how grateful I am now that I had to do this because now my frames are as much fun to make as the paintings themselves.

I have made frames out of lathing, rug scraps, upholstery fabrics, flowers, macaroni, shells, mâché (both paper and sawdust), hardware, typewriter ribbon, almost anything you can mention, and each frame has been a creative adventure.

If you will think for a moment you'll soon come up with dozens of other framing materials.

And that is your next assignment.

ASSIGNMENT NUMBER 6

If you already have some unframed paintings get them out, study them for a while, and make a list of some novel and original ways in which you might frame them.

If you don't have any paintings just get out some wood boards in varous shapes and sizes, or some cardboard or construction paper, or fabric swatches or whatever, and figure out frames for each item.

What Shall I Paint or What Shall I Make?

Let's start with what shall I paint and I'll tell you how I find a subject for a painting. Your method may be quite different. In my former inhibited days I could never decide what to paint and would often sit for hours looking at a blank canvas (and it really was canvas then because I thought it the only thing any respectable artist should use for painting). Frequently nothing would result, or if it did, it was totally unsatisfactory.

Now I just get out paper or wood or anything that looks as if it might make a good background from oil drum tops to plastic container lids, and let my paint brush lead the way with colors flying.

Something unexpected, chuckle-inspiring, or quietly satisfactory almost always results.

It won't be something I set out to make or even thought I could make, and sometimes I can't even identify it. But I always feel better after it's finished. In other words it pleases me. And I ask nothing more. Nor should you.

It may not please your husband or your children or your teachers or your neighbors or your friends or the art critics; it may please no one on earth but you. That's more than enough reason for calling your little effort into being.

This feeling of secret pleasure will provide ample motivation for your next effort and thus will have served its prime purpose: the building of self-confidence.

If you try this method and you find it doesn't work for you be patient, give it time, don't force the issue, just try again. And if nothing happens even when you do try again, here's another little prompter for you.

Don't say to yourself: "Now what should I paint? Should I paint a horse or a flower or a baby or that beach we visited

Contributed by Laura Goodman of Cornell, California, this beautiful wall ornament is made by clipping clothespins to a gilded paper plate and then wiring a bunch of purple plastic grapes to the plate. The clothespins are gilded at the top and the bottoms are painted turquoise, pink, purple, and French blue, alternately.

Sunday?" Nothing good will come of this sort of questioning.

Ask yourself instead: "What are my feelings at this moment? Do I feel happy, sad, mad, bored, lonely, frustrated?" Then ask "How did I feel when my friend told me she had her first baby? How did I feel when my husband brought me those flowers a week ago? How did I feel when I saw that little ghetto child on television? How did I feel when I saw men fighting and dying on the battlefield?"

Questions of this sort will stir your feelings and as you begin to feel, begin to draw or paint. If you are painting don't draw any outlines first. This will freeze you into something that won't be a free expression of feeling at all. Just let colors find their way to each other; allow masses to develop and relate themselves to a whole; speak through your brush and you will be amazed at how articulate it becomes as it speaks for you.

Now let us consider a different process as you answer the question: "What shall I make?" instead of "What shall I paint?"

Here again I can only tell you how I approach the problem. Your solution may be totally unlike mine, but I trust it will be very much like you.

I have a corner where I accumulate "makings." It is a pretty frightening sight to the unitiated and has been described by friends as "organized chaos." Here I can find anything from seahorses, seashells, artificial flowers, nuts, bolts, yarn, wire, wood, paints, scissors and tools, tin snips and jars, to dried leaves, sequins, rick-rack, and marbles. Almost anything animal, vegetable, or mineral on earth is represented here and all uncovered so I can see everything at a glance and don't have to hunt for it.

When I feel the urge to be creative or the desire comes over me to make something that will be different, amazing, or just plain fun, I head for the Makings Corner and just stare at it a while.

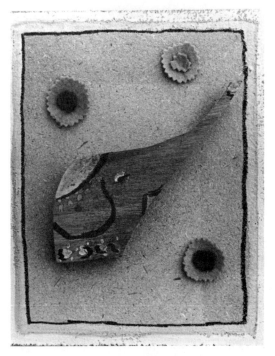

Two wood scraps combine to make this attractive ornament for a child's room. The background is a scrap of pressed wood 8″ x 8″ left its natural beige tone. The "elephant" is another scrap of trim wood stained walnut and decorated with jewels and felt. The flowers are from felt scraps in lively shades of pink, green, yellow, and blue.

The background is a weatherbeaten wood box 19″ wide by 28″ tall and about 4″ deep. Candle boxes (the kind candles are shipped in) were painted glowing orange and sizzling yellow and the designs were clipped from a Christmas card sent us by our local gasoline station—the colors wild blues, purples, reds. Then pieces of broken green glass were stuck in the top of the boxes. The effect, glowing candles against a calm gray ground. Wild and wonderful. Does it suggest something you might like to do with a few discards?

Soon I find myself reaching for things, which I assemble on a tray, and then I take the tray to a quiet sunny spot and go to work. I may or may not have an inkling of what will emerge. If so it is vague, undefined, and extremely nebulous but enough to start me off.

I think I'll make a wall hanging or a plaque or a figurine or a mobile or a gift for someone or just something to prove that art is all around us and design is everywhere.

From there on I let the makings take over, just as I let the paint take over when I embark on a painting. I don't direct; I follow. I enjoy myself. I arrange, change, rearrange and rearrange and before I know it something begins to take shape. Humbly I take direction, obeying some inner command; do it this way, try it that way, never forcing, never getting in the way, just happy about the whole thing.

I never finalize anything the first try, and often not the first day, but set the beginning effort aside and view it with fresh eyes the following day.

Frequently I start several completely unrelated projects in one day and complete them as the spirit moves me. This way I never go stale on them and they never become boring or tedious.

Always I'm amazed at the end result and as surprised as any onlooker might be at what I have brought forth.

Where did it come from? "Where do you get your ideas for these endless creations?" people constantly ask me.

The only honest answer I can give them is that the ideas come to me when I let them. But if I seek them out they evaporate.

It is my firm conviction that ideas will come to you the same way. For all men are endowed equally with creative ability. If I did not believe that, I would never have attempted to write this book. If I had not proved it within my own experience and seen it proved in the experience of others, the book would indeed be a fraud.

But whenever either adults or children have been willing to follow this permissive method, whenever they have strolled through my "makings" and overcome self-consciousness and initial embarrassment, they have invariably made something original, artistic, and pleasing—not only to themselves but to others.

The Desire To Please

Whether we realize it consciously or not, most of us humans spend most of our time and our energy trying to please others. It isn't always an altruistic pursuit, either.

At a time when we're still counting fingers and toes or studying the pattern of the ceiling from our crib we learn to please mother, the great provider of warmth, comfort, and nourishment.

This business of pleasing others to get what you want from them soon becomes a highly developed art. We try to please poppa to get a pat on the head, a piggy-back ride, or a big, booming "You're okay!" laugh.

Soon we try to please our teachers, our bosses, our law enforcers, our husbands and/or wives, our in-laws (if we're in debt to them), our staff sergeant, or the president of the P.T.A.

Yes, the desire to please seems inborn and we have nothing against it. We're a great try-to-please-others kind of person ourselves and we hate to think what the world would be like if most of us didn't try to please most of us most of the time—possibly a great deal worse than it is.

However, there's one place where the desire-to-please can be very harmful and that's in areas of artistic expression.

When you set out to paint or create anything artistic be sure to please only yourself.

That statement summarizes the entire philosophy of this book and we simply can't overemphasize it.

Now of course if you intend to become a professional, commercial, or paid artist you have no choice; you must please your patron, your employer, the person or the organization that pays for your work. Or, as the Spanish people express it: "Whose bread I eat, his song I sing."

But we are talking, in this book, to those who paint or create artistically for love, not for money. You are to please yourself and no one else.

You will find this about the most difficult task you have ever undertaken. For so ingrained is this desire to please that you may find yourself painting or designing things to please others without even being aware that you are doing so.

The only way we know to avoid this is to ask yourself frequently: "Am I doing what I'm doing because I want to; because it satisfies me and I derive pleasure, comfort, and joy from it, or

This is one "Old Saw" that has acquired a new look. We painted it black and anchored it to a board 18″ high by 48″ long and made the corner decorations of black steel file dividers. The background is a wonderful antiqued mixture of blue, white, and gray.

The vase is a little Mexican one of dappled aquamarine glass. The "flowers" are made from the little round perforated tin pieces used as bases for candles. Their stems are florist wire of a gauge that will take a position and hold it. The ethereal beauty of the arrangement is reflected in the subtle patternings of Arnold Wall's sensitive photography.

am I doing it in the hope of winning praise from someone, or approval or commendation?"

The real test will come of the sincerity of your answer when you paint or create something that others do not approve of, that they openly criticize or deride. And your dismay will be magnified a hundredfold if this disapproval or derision comes from someone you love, respect, or admire.

Your confidence will be shaken at a time like this. You will be overcome by doubt and besieged by fear. You will either over-defend your efforts or you will eventually side with the opposition, depending on whether you are inclined to be overaggressive or oversensitive.

This is the subtle, destructive power of praise and the over-whelming, vastly more destructive power of disapproval—when it comes from an awesome, revered personage.

If more parents and teachers would withhold both praise and disapproval at a time when youngsters are just discovering their artistic capabilities, that is, when they first begin to scribble or putter with paint, we would find millions more people capable of enjoying artistic expression and able to release their tensions, hostilities, and joys through the medium of art.

But unfortunately parents and teachers are too often guilty of too lavish praise or too caustic criticism at a time when the budding artist is just beginning to explore the wonders of creativity; thus the bud is forever blighted, never to bloom again.

There is a bright side to this gloomy picture and it is this: more and more teachers are learning how vital it is to let the young artist find himself without the influence of too much praise or too much criticism.

But far too few parents have learned this lesson.

We mentioned earlier, in referring to Viktor Lowenfeld's book *Your Child and His Art,* how important it is to allow the young artist to choose his subject matter, his medium, and his method without direction or interference, and we pointed out how beneficial it is for the parent to accept the child's artistic offering for what it is—an expression of feeling, a reflection of an inner world; not anything that must be understandable to an adult or that must conform to adult standards or, in fact, to any standards except the desires and aims of the creator-artist.

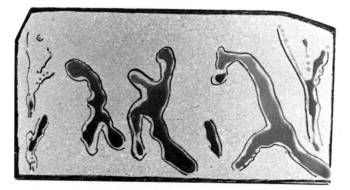

"The Pursuit" is fashioned from candle drippings splashed hit or miss on a pressed wood background, then outlined with black felt pen ink.

The fuzzy ball-fringe "flowers" are actually the droppings from Eucalyptus trees. Dried grass and straw flowers add the right angling and movement to form a united design. The little vase is a discarded perfume bottle. The whole arrangement is about three inches high.

No Need For Straight "A's"

If you are not trying to win anyone's approval for your art and you refuse to be disturbed by anyone's disapproval of it, you don't have to excel at your work; you don't have to be the best non-artist in the neighborhood; your work doesn't have to be outstanding or better than someone else's.

Isn't that a wonderful, comforting thought?

It should relax you and release all your creative energies just to know that the only standard being set for your work is the

Contributed by Donna Killough, of Agoura, California, this exquisitely delicate tableau of the Three Wise Men is made from three date pits and is
contained in a match box 2½″ wide by 5″ tall by 1″ deep. The star of
Bethlehem is a rhinestone, the overhanging branch made from the tiniest
dried wild grass. The Wise Men have seeds for heads, seeds for hats, seeds
for buttons. Truly incontestable proof that art *is* all around us!

standard you set for yourself. If it pleases you it has accomplished
its purpose.

This is such a unique un-American point of view it will probably
come as a shock to you.

From the time we enter grade school we are taught to excel,
to compete, to become outstanding and those of us who don't
excel are labeled failures and shoved to the rear; from then on,
everything we do is open to question, viewed with disapproval,
considered second-best.

No wonder, under such conditions, that the tentative tendrils
of artistic exploration wither and die. They shrink out of sight
and disappear. They remain locked inside and the individual
harboring these locked-in artistic capabilities, these unexpressed
feelings, becomes a frustrated, embittered, failure-ridden, unhappy
member of society.

These are the people we want to reach with a message of hope culled from our own experience.

If you had an artist in the family and you couldn't possibly compete with such excellence; if you had over-criticial or over-adoring parents; if you had neither the time nor the courage for artistic experimentation in your youth; if you were told everything you did must earn a monetary reward or it wasn't worth doing; if you were brought up to believe that artistic pursuits were off-beat, suspect, not socially acceptable; if you were told that you had to have extensive and expensive art training before you could lift a brush or put a stroke on paper, then we want you to know

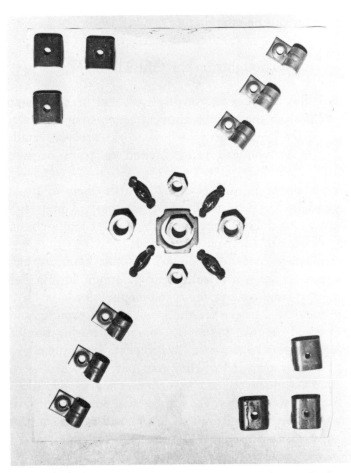

"Art at the Hardware Store" is the title of this design made from toggle bolts, washers, pipe fittings. The colors are black, copper, and silver against a background of beige paper.

that in spite of any or all of these handicaps you can find pleasure in artistic endeavors and, in doing so, became a happier, better integrated person.

You don't have to get straight "A's" for your efforts. You don't have to win praise or approval. All you have to do is turn your back on all the negative conditioning you've had regarding art and decide right now to add a whole new dimension of fun to your life by becoming a devil-may-care non-artist.

ASSIGNMENT NUMBER 7

For this assignment we'd like you to take any collection of articles you may find at hand and make something from them.

It can be something to hang on the wall, stand on a table, place in the patio; it can be anything.

Thoughts on the Old Masters

We will now make a thoroughly rash and heretical statement guaranteed to raise the hackles of every connoisseur-type art lover.

Many of the great masters whose works are venerated today did not paint as you are being invited to paint because they couldn't!

That statement is not meant to belittle their ability, which was tremendous, or their skill, which was just as impressive. As technicians, as masters of composition and color manipulation, and as superb craftsmen they are unexcelled.

But remember that they painted, in most cases, to eat. And we refer now to those who sold their paintings during their lifetime and won fame among their contemporaries.

These men (and where are the women? Performing household tasks that freed the men for artistic pursuits; raising families and making ends meet?) these men, we repeat, very definitely sang the song of their providers. They had patrons. They were commissioned. They delivered art to order. They produced art that could be understood; approved of by the populace: representational, realistic art in depictions of scenes and events, in reproductions of prominent personages; landscapes, seascapes, and "mugscapes" in the popular colors of their day.

This is not art according to our definition, for it is not "Heart Art." It is art of the intellect and the hand; it is skillful maneuvering of materials. But it is not an expression of the artist's inner feeling, of his statement about life; it is not the creation of his imagination; it is not a reflection of the private, one-of-a-kind world in which he finds himself, and, in finding himself, finds a unity with all humanity.

The art of the Great Artists is Art with a capital "A." This is art produced to please the mentors of the times. This is art the art connoisseurs can approve of. You will see these self-styled connoisseurs in galleries around the world, pointing out, in their connoisseur's vocabulary, the beauty of its nuances. This is status art, for which the rich will always pay gladly.

But to my way of thinking this is not true art.

True art is the disapproved of, misunderstood, cast-aside, unsold, and unsought art of the child, the housewife, the downtrodden, and the untaught who, through their paintings, tell us: "The world is a fearful and lonely place and I have lost my way in it." Or, "The world is a joyous and song-filled world and my heart meets yours in it!"

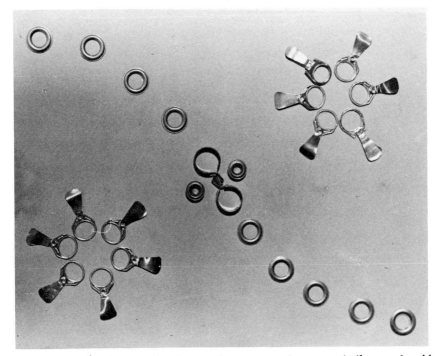

Juice can pull tabs, curtain rings, and grommets, in tones of silver and gold against a bright red ground, form this curvaceous design. Juice can pull tabs also make interesting earrings, hat bands, belts, portieres, café curtains.

True art is the heart poured out on paper; the soul disrobed; the mind exploring itself; the inner world turned inside out. The art of the untrained, the unlearned, the inarticulate, the longing-to-be-listened-to—this is true art.

Art is not esoteric. Art cannot be possessed. Art cannot be confined to a gallery or hung on a wall. Art is for everyone. Art is born in the heart.

Oh. the wonders of Whip-Wax, the creamy-white plastic that you whip to rich consistency, place in a pastry bag, and squeeze out to make all sorts of free-form, fascinating designs. Here the Whip-Wax is left white for the exquisite, ivory-like flowers, tinted yellow to make their brilliant centers and green to form their leaves. The points of the leaves were made by dragging a toothpick through the Whip-Wax before it set. The background is a piece of black scrap boarding which for some reason had the shaded strippings on it that blended so well with the overall design.

ASSIGNMENT NUMBER 8

This assignment might be considered an exercise but it mustn't be brushed aside for that reason, because exercises frequently turn into fun art that becomes the highest example of free-flowing self-expression.

White plastic scraps from a discarded candle mold assembled with flair, fun, and freedom become this engaging conversation piece entitled: "The Party."

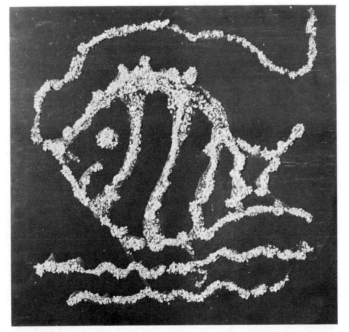

Humble Johnny Cat, usually slated for use in kitty pans, here appears glorified as a lighthearted fish afloat on a board scrap painted black.

Here's the way to set the creative surges in motion: Take a piece of wood, cardboard, or paper of any size, shape, or color. If the background thus selected lacks color, paint it any shade that appeals to you at the moment.

Now take a piece of charcoal or a pencil or a piece of colored chalk or a crayon or dip your brush in paint. The paint may be water color (in which case you may want to work with your background wet); tempera, house paint, oils, or you may wish to work with glue or a mixture of cornstarch and food coloring, or anything else that is available at the moment.

If you're working with charcoal, pencil, chalk, or crayon let your hand drop to the background surface at any point and, with open mind and allowing your hand to lead the way, begin making a design, a pattern, a figure, a scribble, or anything the pencil, chalk, charcoal, or crayon dictates.

If you're working with paint, load your brush generously, drop it to the background surface at any point, and let the color pour off in uncontrolled fashion.

If working with a dry medium, continue to scribble or scrawl till you begin to tire of this action, then set the pencil, charcoal, chalk, or crayon aside and look at the result of your scrawlings in a relaxed and detached frame of mind and see what images project themselves from the background.

If working with paint or other liquid medium, work with one color as long as you enjoy doing so and when you have had enough of that color take up a brush load of another color (or if you would rather dribble or pour on the paint, do so). Don't hesitate about the selection of the second color; choose this color simply because it appeals to you.

Drop this brush load of color to the background surface wherever the hand falls and let the brush create its own design, pattern, or figure against the first color or adjacent to it.

When this color no longer seems to do anything for you or its neighboring color, reach for a brush load of a third color and repeat the action just described. Do not add any more colors.

Now you are ready to sit back in a relaxed and detached frame of mind to observe the results of your efforts. Studying your unstudied creation, what projects itself from the background?

A bird, an animal, a flower, a human form, a building, a tree, a landscape, a child, a repeated pattern, a rhythmic design, or nothing that you can discern?

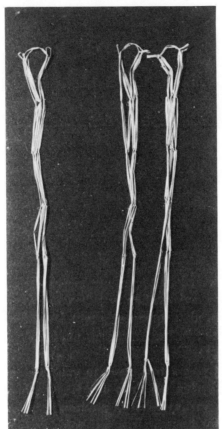

"The Outsider." A rendering from three strands of straw plucked from the basket encasing a wine bottle.

If nothing seems to emerge, turn the painting or drawing this way and that, even upside down, and see what emerges.

Something will certainly emerge if you are patient and persistent. When it does, go to work in your original medium, dry or wet, and take steps to accentuate the emerging form either by heavying up the form itself or blocking in the background.

This lesson in loss of self-control is one of the most valuable creative lessons you can attempt and we hope you will practice doing it at least once a day for an indefinite period.

Save your efforts. Go back to them later. They will tell you remarkable things about your progress, as a person as well as a budding non-artist.

Dramatic evidence of the natural beauty of familiar objects. The design is made from pen points.

Some Asides on Technique

The methods for the development of artistic expression outlined in this book seem so careless and carefree and lacking in serious-minded techniques and methods that many may wonder if more thought shouldn't be given to these weightier and more tangible aspects of art.

To answer your uneasiness on this subject I would like to refer to another book that did so much to help me uncover my own creative possibilities in art that I would like to share some of its precepts with you.

The book I refer to is *The Artist in Each of Us,* by Florence Cane, a woman who taught art for many years at the Center for Gifted Children of the School of Education of New York University, and her book is unique among treatises on the subject of artistic expression inasmuch as it is warm with a love of life and a faith in people that glow through every page.

Mrs. Cane, when asked by inquiring parents and conventional art teachers: "When do you teach technique?" replied: "What do you mean by technique? Isn't it another name for skill? And doesn't skill come from effort and practice? And doesn't the great desire to create form the emotional drive which makes a willingness to labour until skill is attained?"

Mrs. Cane then goes on to say:

"The moment we are taught art, we cease to be artists, and anything real that comes through comes in spite of what we have been taught, rather than because of it. What we need to be taught is not art, but to believe in ourselves, our imagination, our senses, and our hands, to free our bodies and our spirits that we may work and live according to our visions." (Pages 167ff.)

Here is what we are trying to say in this book.

This is what we set out to prove in our personal experience and later we will tell you about certain things that have happened as the result of our personal experimentation and then let you decide whether or not we have proved this principle.

Toward the Liberation of Inhibitions

Mrs. Cane also makes a suggestion in her book for a way to stimulate imagination and liberate creative energy, one that I have tried and found highly effective.

Mrs. Cane worked with many youngsters and adults whom she found were literally living in a state of mental, emotional, and

The background for this hot-dish wall plaque is a pressed wood scrap about 8" x 8" culled from the lumberyard and painted hot orange. The black overlay design of wood is from an unnameable something we picked up at the Salvation Army Outlet Store, which we pasted to the background. The gold hook allows the hot dish pad to hang as an ornament in the patio when not in use.

even physical constriction that caused them to be woefully inhibited not only in their approach to life and to people but also in their approach to art.

Mrs. Cane found that she could un-cramp these emotionally and psychically "knotted-up" individuals by having them go through certain motions and exercises before starting to draw or paint.

She would have them swing their arms, stretch their muscles, bend over, close their eyes, and exhale their breath in a long slow expiration. Then, as they would swing erect, she had them fling wide their arms and sing out with any vowel sound that came to mind, such as ahh, eeeh, oooh, etc.

As her pupils did this they discovered that images came to mind apparently stimulated by the physical and emotional release of this outgoing activity. Different chants or vowel sounds produced different types of imagery. She then had the students paint whatever painting was suggested by this imagery, in whatever colors suggested themselves as appropriate for the mood of the painting.

The results were amazing, and the increase in creativity and

This, the first silhouette I had ever attempted, is cut from a remnant of an old black rubber rain boot I had worn for ten years, which once had belonged to my son. Because of its sentimental value I decided to keep part of it as a memento. The ornamentation is cut from brightly glowing sticky-icky construction paper in fluorescent colors. The background is a discarded cabinet door painted white. The size about 20″ by 20″.

This whimsy, entitled "At the Supermarket," is made from red hots, jelly beans, the spools from two typewriter ribbons, a twist of black plastic covered wire, and a piece of broken car headlight (the base of the carry-cart). The background is a cabinet door painted white, found at the wood shop scrap pile.

the surge of dynamic vitality that appeared in the pupils' work were miraculous.

I tried this method and found it also stimulated me to greater heights of creative effort. But I found I could achieve a similar sense of release and creative exhilaration simply by taking a brisk hike over the hills or romping with the dog or experiencing almost any deep psychic emotion. So the principle here is an appeal to deeper feeling, which always follows the outpouring of pent-up physical energies.

Mrs. Cane also advocated the scribble method I have just outlined to you and found it encouraged the most timid and uncertain artists to take bolder creative strides.

And she employed another creative stimulus that I have used unconsciously in all my art work.

She had the students create a title for and write a little story

The base of this conversation piece is a very old smoking-stand painted mustard gold. A branch anchored with plaster of Paris was painted the same color and adorned with flower-like fungi found in the woods that are brown and leathery. The candles (which are held by nails driven in the wood) are violet and blue. Does this suggest a way for you to turn an old smoking stand into a nameless wonder?

about their finished drawings or paintings. When work is truly creative, not predetermined or directed, this development of a little story to explain the work is invaluable for several reasons. For one thing it clarifies the painting or drawing for the artist. It also permits him to grope for, find, and explain (to himself) the deeper below-consciousness symbolism of whatever he has brought forth.

In doing this the artist uncovers tensions and hostilities long repressed, and achieves an emotional catharsis that tends to integrate his personality and make him easier to live with. In other words, he becomes a happier, better-adjusted person through his art unfoldment.

An antique violin bottle of amber glass becomes a focal point of beauty when used as a container for fragile silver dollar flowers. Arnold Wall's tasteful photography adds the crowning touch of ethereal loveliness.

Art As A Healing Agent

The therapeutic and prophylactic powers of art are no secret, nor are they news, to art teachers, psychologists, and psychiatrists or to any who have done creative rehabilitation work with the lonely, the sick, or the hostile.

Recently a well-known psychiatrist stated that his discovery that art can be a potent healing agent for the emotionally disturbed proved to be one of the most thrilling revelations he had experienced in over twenty years of psychiatric practice.

When his patients painted in an undirected, entirely free and spontaneous manner and were placed under hypnotic trance and. asked to explain what their paintings meant to them they made statements about their work that frequently uncovered the cause of their psychic disturbance.

One woman, as an example, painted some free-form flower patterns in cold, receding colors, that certainly appeared innocuous enough to the casual observer. But under deep hypnosis, when she was asked what her painting expressed with regard to her feelings she said: "They show that nobody listens. Nobody hears me and nobody sees me. It's as if I weren't there. I'm shut out because no one will listen."

The psychiatrist asked her just who it was that didn't listen and she said: "Those I care about," showing a painful and heretofore carefully concealed sense of rejection.

You can use your unfolding artistic expression to improve your health and personality by noting, in the stories you tell about each painting or drawing, what their private significance may be. It is especially helpful, in this connection, to paint or draw while you are thinking back to childhood scenes or earlier experiences or any deeply emotional relationship in your life.

In my own experience I find that I can frequently dispel clouds of worry or gloom and work my way through problems to their solution if I blot out every blast of mental static by becoming completely and happily absorbed in the work at hand.

I also find it helps to increase my interest in my work at the same time that it stimulates interest in others if I give a drawing, painting, or collage a title as I develop it or at its completion. A titled work seems to acquire individuality, stature, and cohesiveness as a result of its captioning. By glancing at some of the illustrations in this book and noting the titles, you will begin, I feel certain, to have a desire to title your own works, and this desire should be encouraged. Do you doubt you have the creative ability to develop original paintings, much less caption them?

Then here's what Alex Osborn, one of the former owners of the famous Advertising Agency of Batten, Barton, Durstin and Osborn, has to say on this subject in his book *Your Creative Power*.

"An analysis of almost all the psychological tests ever made points to the conclusion that creative talent is normally distributed —that all of us possess this talent. The difference is only in degree; and that degree is largely influenced by effort." (Page 118)

ASSIGNMENT NUMBER 9

Let's demonstrate, with this assignment, that you can find art at the sewing center.

Assemble a collection of rickrack, braid, buttons, fabric remnants, upholstery or rug scraps, whatever your sewing kit offers.

Now think what you might make with these bits and pieces.

Consider their color, shape, texture, relationships to one another.

What forms do they suggest? What images come to mind as you look at them?

The unique wall hanging is an old bureau drawer painted white. The flower container is an egg cup likewise painted white. The flowers are blue and red with green leaves. The candles, twists of bright blue beeswax, are displayed in rubber washer "candlesticks" painted red. The floating clouds above the arrangement were cut from bits of the same brilliant blue beeswax.

Devise some sort of background—cardboard or wood or paper in a variety of colors, sizes, and textures. Lay out these backgrounds and then reach for the sewing elements as you feel attracted to them.

Begin to develop an abstract painting or a figure in motion or an animal, flower, building, landscape, or simple design, using elements from your sewing potpourri.

Don't plot or plan, struggle or strain. Let the elements fall into place as they will, proceeding when you are pleased, removing elements that displease you and reaching for substitutes. You may have to arrange and rearrange many times before something takes shape that satisfies you. When this happens begin to paste the pieces to the background with Wilhold Glue. Later you may want to add a frame, or an accent of color, or some crowning touch. For the present, work only as long as you are happy and relaxed.

But Is It Art?

Some visiting, self-imposed art critic is certain to raise this question in viewing what we call art in this book.

The question has convulsed the ages and will continue to do so. It can receive only a personal, search-the-soul answer.

Must it be impressive to be art?

Must it be contained in a costly frame surrounded by its elegant, time-honored peers?

Must the artist be known? Approved? Technically proficient?

Must it command a respectable price in the market?

Must it stand the test of time, thus acquiring the comfortable prestige of the classic?

Must it soothe feelings and not unsettle them?

Must it be readily understandable?

Must it be made of socially acceptable elements and executed by socially acceptable designers?

Must it earn the praise of connoisseur and critic?

Every reader of this book, every would-be artist, every established artist, every art lover, art worshiper, and art collector will answer the above questions differently.

Answer them your way with our blessing.

Here's our answer: It's art if it expresses your feeling in a way that satisfies you and makes you better able to cope with yourself and others.

...ain a cabinet door discarded at our local wood shop makes a perfect back-
...ound and frame for this free-form tree in a stained glass riot of color using
...diant Tempera.

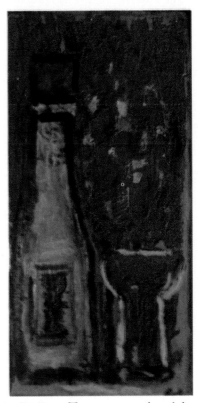

"And Thou," painting on a wood scrap in Radiant Tempera, purchased by
Jack Turley, well-known writer of Television dramas.

"Buttons and Bows," the central design, was made by gluing twelve red
velvet buttons and four vari-colored plastic bows made from candy-wrapping
twists to a background of cardboard.

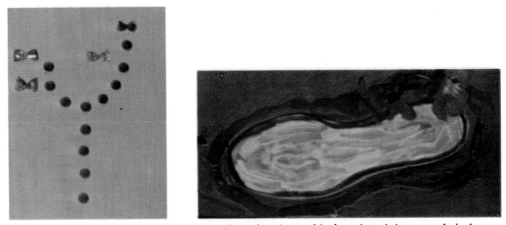

Collage made by gluing the sole of an old shoe found in a creek bed to a
background of masonite and adding a few plastic flowers.

The mermaid and fish are made of candies. The shells are real shells, gilded. The background is a wood scrap 16″ x 24″ painted turquoise. The improvised frame was made by swirling Whip-Wax on the board with free motions of the fingers. Whip-Wax comes in a plastic bottle, may be purchased at craft supply stores. You simply add water, beat with egg beater to whipped-cream consistency, then use for all sorts of decorative designs and frames, freely or squeezed through a pastry tube.

The tree is made of broken glass glued to a plywood panel. The glass anchored to the board for greater security, with antiqued Steelcraft, a decorative black solder, also available in gold and silver that has many exciting artistic uses.

Simulated frame made by painting a color border around a vibrant horse (whose body is made of Johnny Cat, the gravelly substance used in kitty's pan). The saddle and base line are made from colored popcorn (uncooked). The background is a piece of wood stained walnut. Colors are the radiant fluorescent temperas.

"Horse Playing" is a tempera painting on wood. The wood background was glued to a board covered with patterned upholstery fabric and the inner board was outlined with green gift tie yarn. The improvised frame was created by gluing strips of lathe to the outer board and tinting them with burnt umber.

Improvised frame provided by a discarded cabinet door. The central design is made from leaves, pods, and paper strips glued to a walnut-stained ground.

The Bloomin' Tree is painted on a clear plastic sheet and glued to a wood panel. The radiant roses and outspoken leaves and sky make the little tree sing with color.

Here a Christmas card mounted on a wood panel stained brown gives the impression of being framed as the result of a stained glass design, hand painted, that surrounds it.

Experiments with papier mâché in half molds as bas-relief wall plaques. Above, the sea horse is made from our own wood mâché formula, painted with Radiant Tempera, glued to a wood scrap painted yellow and decorated with pink and green gift tie yarn. The bubbles are tiny polished native stones.

Below, the fiddle is made with Celluclay papier mâché glued to a similar board and the flowers were painted on the background in Radiant Tempera.

It's hard to believe that this eye-stopping collection of rhythmic patterns and fascinating textures results from the combination of a piece of bark and some dried pods glued to a scrap of masonite (hung rough side out). The leather thong knotted at the top provides a suitable hanging in the mood of the piece.

About Patterns and Graphs

If you've ever done any craft work or followed any of the instructions for creating art pieces offered through the popular magazines you know how such designs are presented to you.

You are shown the completed work and you are encouraged to copy it.

To help you do this with the minimum amount of effort and

the maximum loss of creativity, you are given a sheet of graph paper or a stencil and told to block out the design, square by square, on the graph paper and transfer it to the surface on which you wish it to appear; or you are invited to copy from a stencil.

This method can do nothing for you except reproduce in your life a copy of someone else's artistic creation. The originator will have the thrill, the release, the pride of accomplishment, and you, for all your painstaking and grubby work, will have a lifeless reproduction that does nothing for you.

You will not master any skill through this sort of manual labor.

At the wood shop scrap pile we found the discarded cabinet door (already painted white) that forms the background for this yarn tree. The colors are moss green, deep rose, and olive green. The "grass" base line is a strip of green fringe.

Sample of an improvised frame made from ordinary white beach shells touched with gold leaf to simulate an antiqued effect. The collage in the center, against a white ground, is made from one large pale blue plastic butterfly and two gold foil butterflies plus a sprinkling of pale plastic violets. The circles enclosing the butterflies are cut from gold foil doilies. Try making an oval or round frame of shells glued to a discarded mirror.

You will not become more artistic nor will you become an artist nor will you produce anything that you can ever say is your own.

It is this sort of copy-craft work that is destroying any spark of creativity or artistic promise that may yet flicker in the heart of those seeking artistic expression.

We are not condemning those who present craft work to the public in this fashion. They know of no other way to present it so

Old bowling pins, thrown out by bowling alleys, become fascinating door-stops, mantel ornaments, and den additions when glued to a heavy wood base, spray painted flat black—rich and velvety—and decorated in the diplomatic manner with a green grosgrain ribbon, a red velvet bow, and a topaz crowned jewel (culled from an old house slipper). Bowling enthusiasts may add a gold plaque at the bottom for personal glorification.

that Mrs. X, who (thinks she) is totally without artistic ability, and who has never done any sort of art work in her life, may imagine, on seeing a finished copy of someone else's creative endeavor, that she suddenly has become artistic.

It would be far better, however, to present the finished art sample to the reader and then tell her to use it as an inspiration for her own design. Let her color it in her own way. Let her frame it or not frame it as she sees fit. And then, though the final result might be far less perfect and perhaps totally different from the original, at least it would be the creation of Mrs. X.

Mrs. X would get a thrill out of it and would be encouraged to try other efforts on her own. But as long as she copies anything she will never advance beyond her present stage of timid self-constraint.

Your design, your colors—however crude, however primitive, however unconventional and imperfect—are far more exciting, far more rewarding, than any designs or colors created by skilled artists or craftsmen—because they're YOURS!

So, please, please don't use stencils. They're as damaging to the budding artist as outline color books. And please, please don't use graph paper to plot your designs. You'll never have anything but wooden lifeless nothings if you do. This is fine for those who have to do commercial art or who must produce for public consumption. But you are going to do everything freehand, boldly, blithely in your own way and in doing so you will express your own artistic ability.

More About Freedom

The freer the person, the freer the art; the freer the art, the freer the person. It's a sort of interlocking psychic cycle. And since it's more difficult to free the artist than to free his art, we're starting with the art. It worked that way for us so we like to believe it will also work for you.

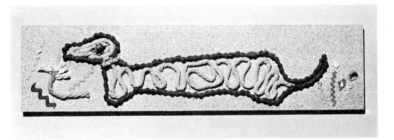

A scrap of pressed wood twenty-six inches long by eight inches wide left its natural beige color is the background for this delectable dachshund made from a richly rusted bicycle chain. Brilliant orange gift tie yarn forms the body, rickrack in turquoise, green, and violet the surrounding flowers; the eye is an emerald-green bead.

When you're drawing or painting must a face look like a face or a tree a tree? Must bodies and houses and backgrounds and other objects be correctly positioned and ideally proportioned?

We've really answered these questions in earlier portions of this book but we bring them up again and amplify the answers at this point because we want to remove every last lingering doubt on this score. The answer is NO to all those questions.

As we have tried to make clear all the way, distortion is a very important aid to creative expression. You draw arms, faces, any object, as you feel about it.

Artistic selectivity determines what is important and deserving of emphasis at the same time that it determines what is irrelevant and therefore to be diminished or cast aside.

Abstract the essence of any object, its basic curve or line or sweep or movement, its extracted feeling, and the observer will contribute the details. Let the observer do this. To supply every particular is to produce the dull and the obvious—is really to insult the viewer by imagining that he is incapable of making a contribution.

The imaginative contribution that you make to art as a viewer is actually that which endears it to you.

ASSIGNMENT NUMBER 10

Using any type of background you prefer, in any color that appeals to you, dip your paint brush in any color that sustains your interest and—USING AS FEW LINES AS POSSIBLE AND SUPPLYING AS FEW DETAILS AS POSSIBLE— paint a bird, a tree, a house, a flower, a horse, a cat, a dancer, a landscape.

Remember, in drawing or painting any subject, you will unconsciously distort, either through overemphasis or underemphasis, that which you fear, crave, love, or hate. Let this happen and your art will have free-flowing, unfettered vitality.

Also, black and white is intellectual, color is emotional. When working with color allow your color choice and your color emphasis to run the entire range of your deepest, most urgent emotions.

ASSIGNMENT NUMBER 11

This is an exercise in imagination stimulation.

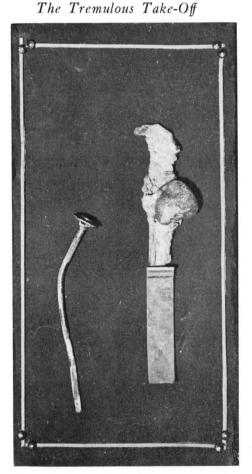

"The Candidate" is a whimsy made by gluing a very large bent nail and two rusted pieces of scrap iron to a board painted flat black. The board measures 8½ x 18″. The improvised frame is made by gluing brown strips of leather thong in place and adding two bronze ornamental upholstery tacks at each corner.

Think back to your childhood, to your tenderest or most fearful memories, and express your feelings about these memories by allowing your unguided hand to paint freely on a large area as you let thoughts come to the surface.

Here is another facet of this exercise in imagination stimulation.

Think of things that you have long desired but never quite attained. Things you have truly longed for most of your life.

Thinking thus deeply, allow your hand, without direction, to

You'll never win the sixty-four thousand dollars trying to guess what this little tree (exactly four inches high) is made from. The base is a broken spring to which we attached a plastic dove. The tree itself is a piece of tree branch but the lace-like willowy foliage is made from aluminum strands of radar tracking material that dropped from a plane on a neighbor's ranch. The tree and base and bird are gold, the radar strands sparkling silver.

create designs on any backgrounds of your choice. Be sure your choice of background color and working colors is automatic. Select always the color that says: "I'm the one. Work with me!"

Another imagination prompter: Cover a sheet of paper with a film of water or mineral oil or even egg white mixed with water or glue mixed with water. Be sure the paper or background surface is not absorbent so your liquid surface film will remain fluid.

While the surface film is still liquid, dip your brush in colors without premeditation and draw the brush through the pliant film.

All sorts of strange and wonderful things will appear as you do this. If you use an oily background liquid and work with water colors or tempera, the oil will resist the water and create even more remarkable effects. (Clean brushes well after this experiment or you may have difficulty when you switch to a later medium.)

As the strange underwater-type shapes appear, stop every so often to decide, in your mind, what is appearing. Is it a flower, a fish, a tree, an abstract, a mood? Whatever it is, don't bring it to completion but leave it in its first nebulous beginnings and let your imagination fill in the missing details.

Keeping Feeling Alive

We have said repeatedly that art is an expression of feeling. What happens to artistic expression then, when genuine feeling is allowed to atrophy? The answer is more than evident in the scarcity of feeling-art or heart art, as we call it.

We are often accused of becoming a nation of people without feeling, and in far too many instances this accusation is justified. We don't wish to place the blame for this national numbness. In fact, how could we? But we will say this. We fear that much loss of spontaneous, outgoing responsive feeling among both children and adults is occasioned by the brutality and violence depicted on television and on the motion picture screen.

The viewer, whether a child or an adult, who is exposed to this continuous onslaught of mayhem has only two choices: either to become a seething, sensitive sounding-board of emotion, or a frozen, unfeeling automaton.

In self-defense the citizenry has apparently settled for the latter choice. You can't watch death on the battlefield or on the movie set, in your living room, month after month after month, without building some sort of mental resistance.

The unfortunate extension of this blocking of natural emotional response is that eventually we become unfeeling in our relationship to our fellow humans and less concerned for their welfare, and finally we find ourselves devoid of feeling.

This unhappy state may frequently be corrected through persistent practice at undirected artistic expression. Soon the feeling breaks through, comes to the surface, flows to the paper, and creative energies begin to liberate the numbed psyche. The artist

The beauty—stark, simple, compelling, dramatic—of a discarded bicycle gear painted flat black and ornamented with a single topaz stone at its center. Now it can be hung on the wall of den or boy's room to astonish and delight all beholders.

is able to express feeling in his art and now he begins to express feeling in his personal contacts with others. He becomes more human and at the same time more humane.

More sensitive to his own needs and therefore more sensitive to the needs of others. More aware of the cruelty and the tenderness in the world and more capable of sublimating the cruelty and amplifying the tenderness on canvas and in his human relations.

And so we advise you, do as little thinking and as much feeling as possible when you attempt to express yourself through any artistic medium.

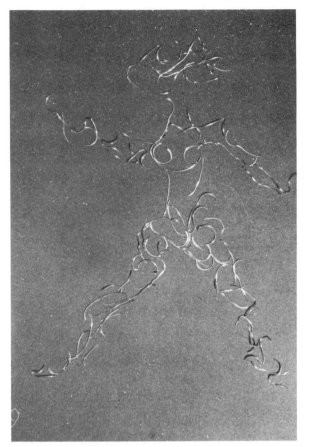

To remove the pages from a spiral looseleaf notebook I found it necessary to cut the wire spiral at frequent intervals. Looking at the silvery fragments I realized they were vibrant with design possibilities. I dropped them on a piece of black construction paper, pushed them about with a forefinger, this way and that, and the dynamic female figure that you see here assumed its dramatic stance.

Don't look outside for objects to draw. A camera could do a much better job of reproducing reality than you could. So could a draftsman. But you are to look within you for ideas for your paintings, for the source of designs, for creative stimulation.

Your memory of the way a tree looks, the way a river flows, the way a horse prances, or the way a clown smiles is your feeling about these experiences. Why draw them otherwise?

Feel big, work big—or at least at the bigness most comfortable for you. Are you patient or impatient? Looking for the beauty of microscopic details or craving the whole world for your canvas?

Draw your way, paint to your scale, create at your pace—it's the only way to grow.

Does music help you? Does it release your inhibitions, stimulate your emotions? Then by all means use music as a background when you create. Wordless, preferably, or the words may get in the way of your mental images. Let the music suggest moods, rhythms, colors, and masses to you and allow these promptings to pour forth in free-flowing, uninhibited designs. The results will astonish and delight you.

But above all, be active. Walk, dance, swim, play, then create. Creative energy is stimulated and released by physical and mental activity; it becomes inactive and dries up when you are inactive.

But don't try to work at your art when you are tired. Tiredness shows up in your work as complexity. Freshness leads to simplicity and openness and reflects a fresh and open mind.

ASSIGNMENT NUMBER 12

Take a walk along the beach or somewhere in the country (it should be possible for everyone to find some time and some way to do this) and enjoy the experience, looking for every detail of beauty and interest that you can find.

Drink in the beauty of sky, sea, and trees, of scents and sounds, of space and quietness.

Bring home as many happy memories and new feelings as you can, and also bring home as many natural oddities as you can collect—bark, leaves, seed pods, dried flowers, grasses, pebbles, rocks, sea shells, naked branches, anything that appeals to you.

As soon as you can after this field trip make several drawings and paintings, from memory, expressing your feelings about what you saw.

Work in any medium on any background and in any combination of colors that pleases you and seems best to express your emotions.

Then make some original designs or creations, using the things that you collected while on your trip.

Bolstering Budding Bravado

Sorry if we seem to get personal at this time. There's a reason. It's to bolster your budding bravado by telling you about the

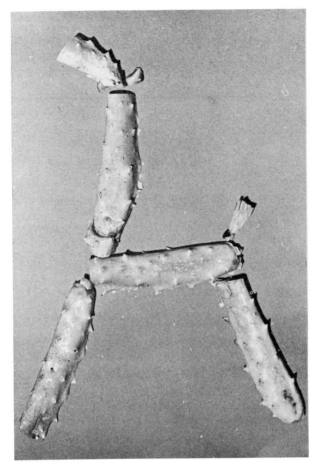

Made from the legs of king crab, this rosy-pink giraffe is glued to a background of dark green construction paper. Unless you live where king crab is available you may have to experiment with other forms of crustacea. You can also make beautiful wind chimes from crab legs. See if you can figure out how it's done.

wonderful things that have happened to us since we threw caution to the culture vultures and decided to fly it our way.

Before long friends and neighbors began dropping in to look at our artistic efforts. This is the most critical point in the life of a non-artist, which is why we want to prepare you for it.

People who view your beginning artistic creations will usually fall in one of three well-defined categories:

1) Those who are overwhelmed and astonished to think that little old you produced all these marvels. They will be profuse in

their praise (even though secretly horrified at your abandon, your color madness, your often, to them, totally inexplicable paintings). People in this category will insist they could never in a lifetime attempt to do anything artistic since they have no artistic ability and absolutely no artistic training.

These are the people for whom this book is written, for these are the people who need it most. They need to be led patiently and understandingly to the point where they will at least try to overcome their inhibitions through artistic experimentation.

2) The second category of viewers of your art work contains those who are really shocked and horrified by your efforts and don't mind saying so. They will tell others (but not you) that you are a pitiable case, for you haven't really produced anything that faintly resembles "art" that your colors are sickening, your work madness. Sometimes these people will remain friendly with you.

3) The third category of self-appointed critics of your work includes the so-called art connoisseurs. These are the worshipers of "Art" with a capital "A." They read all the art reviews they can lay hands on; they visit all the art museums and status art galleries and "in" private art exhibitions.

The members of this group may be too kind to express any opinion of your work audibly, but they will hold it in the greatest contempt. They will say there is no art without formal training and only those born with artistic ability can hope to become artists. They will hold the artistic "greats" up as examples of what may be considered legitimate art. They will compare your work with the old masters and the comparison will shrivel your courage to nothingness.

If you hide your work in a back room and never show it to anyone outside your immediate family you can avoid all these traumatic comments but we don't advise you to do this.

We'll tell you what we did and what happened then you can see what steps you'd like to take regarding the public exposure of your little soul children.

The "I" of the Beholder

Herb Grosswendt, the gentleman who manages the local winery in our area, asked to hang some of my art work on display there in order to brighten up the place—a vast cavernous structure done in the dark awesome tones of the early missions. The winery is a

Three little dried grass arrangements, the tallest less than six inches high. The one on the left is in a tiny vial glued to a walnut-stained woodblock. The center one is a dried branch anchored in a steak bone; bone and branch gilded and ornamented with tiny silver and pale green beads. The right-hand bottle is deep green, with a gold plaque hung around its neck, trimmed in French blue. The board base is also painted French blue.

headquarters for many social events of the community because of its size and accessibility.

Much to my astonishment and delight, the paintings began to sell. To me this seemed the miracle of the ages. To think that someone would actually pay cash for something I had done for pure fun!

I thought the paintings should be priced very low, not only so that those who really wanted to enjoy them could afford to do so, but also because I felt they couldn't possibly be worth much. I would put a low price on the paintings and my benefactor and patron, the manager of the winery, would mark them up. When I returned to look at the paintings again—something I did often because the sight of these little nothings hanging there so bravely in public fed my soul with heavenly manna—I would find that my good friend had marked the paintings up again. And the wonder

Madonnas of many moods, each cut from a Christmas card, glued to a wood scrap, then sprayed with clear plastic. The central arched piece is painted flaming pink as a joyous deviation for the very modern Holy Family.

of it was that he would always sell them at the marked-up price.

"But I only make these things out of odds and ends, for fun, and I'm no artist, never having had an hour's formal art instruction in my life!" I protested. "So you mustn't charge much for my work."

My friend taught me a valuable lesson in his reply. He explained that I was not selling materials or even time, since most things I made very quickly, but I was selling two priceless commodities for which people will pay: Imagination and joy.

"Where else could anyone find a duplicate of your work?" he demanded.

Where else indeed? He silenced my desire to give away my paintings and I let him price them from then on and he continued to sell them.

Professional Competition

Next came a test.

In fairness to other talent in the community, the manager of the winery decided to invite other artists to exhibit their works on a rotation schedule. And, since my paintings weren't taking up very much room in the tremendous building, he let them remain.

My heart quaked. I was confident I'd never sell another painting. I had seen some of the paintings of the first artist whose works would be in competition with mine and they were so magnificent, so polished and perfect, so excitingly beautiful, so professional, that they made my wild colors and outlandish whimsies seem blatant, banal, brash—rankly amateurish. I wanted to remove my paintings so they wouldn't have to face this staggering competition, but to do so would have seemed ungracious. So I let the

The background for this low key, mellow wall plaque is the end of an ancient wooden box stained walnut. The opening at the right was the hole by which the box was carried. The praying hands, cast in brown wax, were glued to the background and anchored with a strip of rugged brown leather held in place with decorative brass upholstery tacks. Two pink paper roses, very old and faded, provided just the proper touch of piety and promise.

paintings remain, but I stayed away for the entire month that the other artist's paintings were on display.

When I finally worked up sufficient courage to return, I learned that this professionally trained artist had sold only one painting, but during the same period four of my paintings had sold!

I was overwhelmed! This man had been a commercial artist many years, had exhibited his work here and abroad, had won many coveted art awards, and when he did sell a painting it brought, at the least, hundreds of dollars. What was the answer? Why did my amateurish doodlings sell?

My good benefactor and patron, Herb Grosswendt, was once

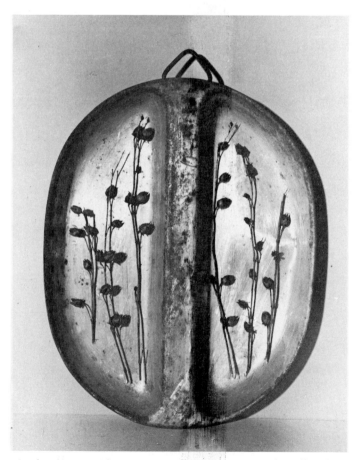

One of the loveliest accidents ever to happen to us artistically. A very old prospector's mess kit, contributed by Carol Boynton, is here left "as is" and simply decorated with delicate strands of dried seed pods.

again kind enough to point out the reason: "You are selling joy and imagination, remember? Not skill or technique or slickness or polish, but heartbeats and love of life and surging, singing color that is pouring out of you because for the first time in your life you're letting it pour out. People will buy sincerity, they will buy freshness and wit, they will buy what their eye beholds on your canvas. Keep painting."

And so I did. And as I did here's what happened. A very famous art director of a nationally known television film company saw some of my work and bought a painting—which would have

Please do not ask me, for I know not what it is. I refer to the black, wrought iron ornament anchored to the walnut stained discarded drawer panel. The stem is made from charcoal sticks and snips of black shiny patent leather. The size of the mysterious black rose: 4½" by 36".

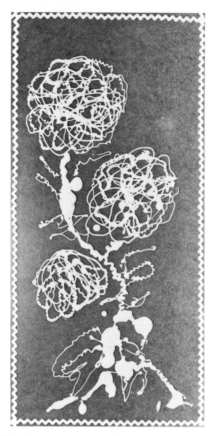

These frothy lace-like flowers were made by trailing white Whip-Wax from a pastry tube onto a large board, 18″ wide by 38″ high, stained walnut. White rickrack forms the just-right zig-zag border.

been enough to delight any beginning non-artist. But in addition he said he thought I had promise, real ability, and should be exhibiting my paintings at a major gallery, where he felt certain they would sell.

Next an art instructor from UCLA and one from another local college saw my work and stated it was original and fresh and full of artistic vitality.

Other art teachers dropped by and bought some of my paintings. All of these people said I should be exhibiting at a major gallery.

Would I do this, my benefactor wanted to know?

I gave this a great deal of thought. After all, the possibility of fame, fortune, or even mild and modest exposure is tempting to any would-be artist. And I certainly needed the material rewards. I have to do all my painting on scraps, with scraps, and have never invested any money in conventional paints, brushes, canvases, or frames.

A Decision and Its Rewards

I finally made my decision: not to exhibit my work.

I reasoned this way: I set out to prove that anyone who is willing to try can become a successful non-artist, enjoying the thrill and the satisfaction of uninhibited artistic expression. My premise all of the way has been that you achieve this artistic freedom by painting or creating to please yourself and no one else; by not following any of the established rules and by not subjecting yourself to any formal art training.

I had proved my point.

But, if I were to go further; if I were now to try to become an artist, quotes, caps, by the world's standards, I would have to please others; I would have to think of others' opinions—unconsciously if not consciously. I would inevitably travel down the path

The background board is stark white. A cigar box cover painted deep scarlet is anchored to this background with gold upholsterer's tacks. The central ornament is a gold foil gift wrap emblem. The outer border consists of tiny strips of red plastic tape with three red beads at each corner. The completed wall plaque has a rich and regal impact, striking against dark green wallpaper.

Convincing evidence that ART *IS* ALL AROUND US. One corner of the author's studio where more than a hundred (count 'em) "creations" bear witness to the fact that design is everywhere and beauty in the eye of the beholder.

to professionalism. This was a path I had followed in writing that I did not wish to follow in art. I decided to continue to have fun as a free and unfettered non-artist!

And what happened when I made this decision?

Through word-of-mouth comments people began to hear of my work; they started to drop in to see it. My workroom soon acquired the name of a "studio," people asked to buy the things they saw there, and so I am able to create things and to paint, just as I please, when I please, and face the prospect of a nice little income that will certainly more than pay for my hobby. Could a non-artist ask for more? I doubt it.

Go Thou and Do Likewise

And so I say to those of you who have followed, timorously or even skeptically, the precepts and the promise contained in this little book: Go thou and do likewise!

For you there must be no concern with balanced compositions; no regard for rhythmic repetitions of lines or patterns; no struggling with planned color harmonies; no agonies of self doubt or self criticism. For you there must be only derring-do, freedom, and fun.

To a child, art is play and we say keep it that way.

Make a display board and rotate your paintings on it. And don't hang your efforts where they will be expected to compete with the work of professionals—at least not until your confidence reaches a point where you can do this without feeling that your work should be turned to the wall.

Visit contemporary local art displays as often as you can to see what other beginning artists are doing.

And take time, now and then, to lie fallow. If you become as deeply and satisfactorily involved in art as I have, you will find you can scarcely tear yourself away from your experimentations and explorations, but you must. Stay away from your paints, brushes, and "makings" for a few days and you will come back to them with new eagerness, freshness, and resolve.

But if you should find that you pumped the creative well dry from overzealousness, do not despair. It will prime itself and whole new springs of creativity may be tapped if you simply break up your daily routine for a day or two. Visit a new place and absorb its sights and sounds. Or, if you can't get away, switch to a new medium. If you've been working in tempera, try water color. We said earlier that water color is a difficult and sometimes discouraging (because evasive) medium for the beginner. But, conversely, water color can be a liberating and stimulating medium if you don't strive for immediate perfection.

Work with a wet background, let color flow freely from your brush; deep, rich, impact colors—no whispery, delicate hues—and as the beautiful fringes of overlapping color fan out and intermingle in unsought-for, intricate designs, allow the color patterns to create their own subject matter; let them evolve their own designs and then encourage your imagination to title what you have created.

Sometimes it is stimulating to turn away from paint entirely for a brief interval and investigate the compelling beauty of stitchery—today's modern pictorial needlework.

The art of painting with stitches involves much more than the use of needle and thread. You can work with yarn, twine, straws, toothpicks, shells, etc., on backgrounds of tarleton, burlap, paper, cardboard, or hardwood. One technique lets you pour hot wax on the hard wood, then you press your yarn into the wax while it is still warm to make your design.

Of course, in working with stitches, the aim is to be as freely creative as you would be with any other medium. No pre-drawn designs, please. No pre-conceived notions of what must develop as you start stitching.

Simply select a background that pleases you, assemble a variety of yarn, thread, or whatever in colors that stimulate you, and let an image form in your mind. Is it a peacock, an octopus, a mermaid, an abstract or geometric pattern, or is pure color leading the way? As color or yarn calls to you, reach for it, stitch or glue it to the background—whichever suits your mood—and watch the most wondrous things evolve.

A fabulous book on this subject, entitled *Stitchery Art and Craft* by Nik Krevitsky, will open up a whole new world for you in this fascinating, little-explored realm of fabric and thread painting.

And in his book Mr. Krevitsky makes a statement I'd like to pass along to you. He says: "Artists have been affected by the new sciences of cybernetics and bionics; they have been influenced by data processing, multi-media communication, and by atomic fission, these developments all leading to the many new art expressions which depict break-up, fragmentation, compartmentalization, isolation, and a reorganization of the complex contemporary world." (Page 86)

There is much to think about here: a whole source of new imagery and subject matter that will lead you into a world of present and future artistic exploration. Designs and patterns drawn from these subjects speak to our contemporaries. They also enliven art, giving it immediacy and power, and distract us from the cloying cuteness and vapid sentimentalism of the past. This does not mean that there isn't a place for nostalgia and backward looks. We simply mean that the artist must express his own feelings, his own relationship to life, and he will do this if he creates to please himself and does not try to curry popular favor.

Importance of Your Own Art Collection

It is important that you make your own art collection and just as important that you keep adding to it. It may consist of paintings, collages, works of découpage, figurines, antiques, natural oddities, prints or reproductions of old masters or present-day artists, and of course the work of beginning artists of today.

Anything should go into your collection that you love; that speaks to you in a private, special way. My own collection includes articles of every texture, size, shape, and color. Wood, metal, leather, fabric, rocks, shells, branches, paintings, almost anything you can name, are represented. These treasures do more for me in a creative sense than I can possibly say, because they inspire me to emulate them. Your collection should do the same for you.

3

By Way of Summary

Have we given you the courage to try?

That's all we set out to give you. The rest is already yours. The love of life, the love of people, the desire to seek, to explore, to experiment are a part of you. Nurture them, cherish them, share them, always keeping within mind this thought: To paint with the eye and the hand without the heart is to accomplish nothing, however clever or correct the result.

We preach not art for art's sake, but art for love's sake.

Love your work and others will love it.

Love your work whether others love it or not!

If there are unloving or unlovely feelings that must be expressed, by all means express them. Art doesn't have to be sentimental to be true art, but very definitely it must be honest.

As I neared the completion of this book my workshop was filled with more than three hundred designs, paintings, figurines, bibelots, and unnameable creations that had evolved in the course of its development.

People entering it would gasp in astonishment and refuse to believe that one person could be responsible for such an outpouring. They gasped again and became even more incredulous when I explained that less than eighteen months had elapsed since I took my first step toward artistic expression. Before that time I had never made anything on my own, had never painted or sketched or done any work of a similar nature, and I was absolutely untrained.

I tell you this for only one reason: What I have done you can do.

And, as you become more artistically confident, you will find that your emerging appreciation of art will enrich your life in many unexpected ways.

You'll begin to dress more artistically, with greater color freedom, with more verve and vitality.

You'll cook more artistically, with more attention to the blending of colors and flavors, more concern for the artistic presentation of food to your family.

You'll also decorate your home more artistically.

New colors will sing and surge through it. New forms, masses, arrangements will appear. And these exciting new decorative touches will express your personality, you special taste; not your neighbor's or your mother's, or the taste of the mass manufacturers or the tastemakers.

But the final, most thrilling result comes when you begin to think as an artist and to live as an artist, to find design and beauty everywhere.

This is when you make the transition from "Non-Artist" to true artist; when the glorious heart-pounding realization bursts upon you that art IS all around us, and, more importantly, that art is also within us—to inspire us, comfort us, and unite us in a wonderful interrelatedness—world without end.

Bibliography

Creative Teaching in Art, Victor d'Amice, International Textbook Co., 1955
Through Art to Creativity, Manual Barkan, Allyn & Baker, 1960
The Artist in Each of Us, Florence Cane, Pantheon Books, 1951
Children Are Artists, David Mendelowitz, Stanford University Press, 1953
Exploring Paper Mâché, Victoria B. Betts, Davis Press, 1956
Creative Hands, Doris Cox and Barbara Warren, John Wiley & Sons, 1951
Collage and Construction, Lois Lord, Davis Publications, 1958
On Vital Reserves, William James, Henry Holt
The People and the Painter, Claire Fejes, Knopf
Your Creative Power, Alex Osborn, Scribners
Abstract Art, Frederick Gore, Crown Publishers, 1966
Stitchery—Art and Craft, Nik Krevitsky, Reinhold, 1966
Creative and Mental Growth, Viktor Lowenfeld, Macmillan.
Your Child and His Art, Viktor Lowenfeld, Macmillan, 1954
Exploring with Paint, Petterson and Gerring, Reinhold, 1964
The Psychology of Children's Art, Rhoda Kellogg and Scott O'Dell, CRM
   —Random House, 1967
Primer of Perception, Jennifer D. Wymar and Stephen F. Gordon, Rein-
   hold, 1967
The Complete Book of Découpage, Frances S. Wing, Coward McCann, 1965
Collect, Print and Paint From Nature, John Hawkinson, Whitman, 1963
Direct Metal Sculpture, Meilach and Seiden, Crown, 1966
Model Making, George Aspden, Reinhold, 1964
Shell Art, Helen K. Krauss, Hearthside Press, 1965
Resin and Glass Artcraft, Lura Smith, M. Barrows, 1966
Make Things with Straw & Raffia, Jutta Lammer, Watson-Guptill, 1965
Sculpture and Ideas, Michael F. Andrews, Prentice-Hall, 1966
Applique—Old and New, Nedda C. Anders, Hearthside Press, 1967
Make Your Own Gifts, Jutta Lammer, Watson-Guptill, 1964
Fun with Metalwork, J. W. Ballinger, Bruce Publishing Co., 1958
Make Your Own Costume Jewelry, Jutta Lammer, Watson-Guptill, 1965
Make It in Paper, Michael Grater, Mills & Boon, Ltd., London, 1961
Crafts & Hobbies, Garry Winter, ed., Arco Publishing Co., 1964
Creative Crafts Magazine, P. O. Drawer C., Ramsey, N. J. 07446

Sources of Supplies

American Handicrafts, 1001 Foch Street, Fort Worth, Texas 76107
American Wax Corp., Azusa, Calif.
Bersted's Hobby Craft, Inc., Monmouth, Illinois.
Generals Supplies Co., P. O. Box 338, Fallbrook, Calif. 92028
Home-Sew, Inc., 1825 West Market St., Bethlehem, Penna. 18018
Ideas Unlimited, Graff Pub., Inc., 910 N. Marshfield, Chicago, Illinois
Pack-O-Fun, Scrap Craft Magazine, 1 Main St., Park Ridge, Ill. 60068
Celluclay Co., Inc., Marshall, Texas
Craftint Manufacturing Co., 18501 Euclid Ave., Cleveland, Ohio 44112

And your local craft and hobby supply store.